Bob Acton

THE LANDFALL
OF THE
POLDICE V.

Wheal Fortune (Cusvey M~~u...~~), ~~walk~~ +

WHERE IS IT?

The area covered by this book ranges from Penpol, between Feock and Devoran, in the east, to Carn Marth, near Redruth, in the west and Chacewater in the north. The focal point is the valley between Crofthandy and Todpool where one of Cornwall's greatest mines, Poldice, was situated, and the recommended starting point of all the routes described is the entrance to that valley now named Wheal Unity Gate. This is a short distance east of the centre of St Day, and is a turning off the minor road running north from Crofthandy towards Chacewater. The Ordnance Survey grid reference is SW 737429. Although the sketch maps in the book should be adequate to prevent you from losing your way, I strongly recommend you to supplement them with the relevant OS maps, namely Landranger 204 (Truro/Falmouth), which covers the whole area apart from Carn Marth, or ideally Pathfinder 1360 (Truro), which omits only Devoran, Point and Penpol.

First published 1990
by
LANDFALL PUBLICATIONS
Landfall, Penpol, Devoran, Truro, Cornwall TR3 6NW
Telephone: Truro (0872) 862581

Copyright © R. S. Acton 1990

A CIP catalogue record for this book is available
from the British Library.

ISBN 0 9514517 8 2

USING THIS BOOK

Unlike my main series of walks books, this one has sections you need to
sit down and read, but it is also a book to take out with you and use.
You will find suggestions for very short walks around Poldice Mine and its
immediate surroundings; two "medium" walks of about 3 miles; four longer
walks; and two routes better suited to cyclists and horse-riders. They are
all "circular" routes. Since the book deals with a relatively small area,
the walks and other routes overlap, so to avoid having to repeat some
"background" information several times I have concentrated the bulk of it
in boxed notes included in the directions for the four longer walks.
Comments on practicalities such as places of refreshment, likely conditions
under foot, and so on, are also mainly attached to those four walks, in the
italicised introductory notes. The starting / ending place for every walk
and ride is the Wheal Unity Gate entrance to the Poldice Valley (although
alternatives are also given in a few cases). This is because the Poldice
Valley Trust hopes to build a car park there for visitors to the Valley.
Until that comes about, however, there is not much room for parking at
that point, and you may need to try one of the other entrances such as
Poldice Gate or Crofthandy Gate, or find a place where roadside parking is
safe. Guidance for finding Wheal Unity Gate and details of recommended OS
maps are given in the note on the title page, overleaf.

Bob Acton, November 1990

Typesetting, maps, drawings and photographs by Bob Acton,
unless otherwise stated

Printed by Century Litho, Penryn, Cornwall

*DRAWING ON BACK COVER: The castle-like ruins of Poldice Mine arsenic works
as seen from Todpool Gate. The attractive sign is one of a series painted
by Ron Collins of Tailings End, Goongumpas.*

PREFACE

Events in Cornwall in the 18th century were as important as anywhere else in the world for stimulating the events which led to the Industrial Revolution. There are some who say that the steam engine was invented because of Cornish mining activities. Poldice Valley played a leading role in these events, as this short book hopes to illustrate.

Despite its remarkably prominent and well documented role in Cornish affairs the Poldice Valley environment had by the late 1980s entered into a downward spiral of mistreatment resulting in public meetings being held in Truro and Crofthandy. From these and with the generous financial assistance of the following companies:

E. Thomas Construction   T. C. Engineering
T. H. Douce & Sons   Liscorvah Sawmills
Practical Developments   Hendy's Carpets
Tony Craze Fabrication & Steelwork Massie Ludnow & Jenkins

the Poldice Valley Trust was formed with the aims of preserving and where necessary restoring the valley landscape and heritage. Gwennap Parish Council have from the outset given full support and encouragement and I am pleased to say are actively involved in the Trust's affairs.

British Gas plc made generous provision for pipeline restoration at the western end and assistance in the work of the Trust has subsequently been received from the Cornwall Rural Community Council and Shell GB. Government assistance has been forthcoming from the Department of the Environment and the Countryside Commission. Kerrier Groundwork Trust with the help of a grant from Carrick District Council have from day one provided practical help resulting in major initial improvements. The so-called "Green Machine" caterpillar digger worked free of charge, courtesy of Finning Ltd, for several weeks and major improvements have already been secured.

The Trust is indebted to the many landowners who are co-operating in this project.

This book is not an attempt to provide the authoritative work on the area as limitations of budget preclude such an undertaking. However I hope it shows the importance of the valley and that it does provide a valuable resource for educational as well as recreational uses. There is even scope for archaeological study on a professional scale for those intent on finding old "Atmospheric" Engine sites and similar antiquities.

Who could condense everything and still make it coherent and enjoyable? Bob Acton, author of so many small books on Cornwall, seemed the right choice for a "proper job" and I hope readers will enjoy his work as much as I have in the proof reading.

D.H.Lanyon
Chairman Poldice Valley Trust
October 1990

INTRODUCTION

My interest in the Poldice Valley and its immediate neighbourhood was aroused in 1988 when I began researching the first "Landfall Walks Book", *A View from Carn Marth*. When Chris Massie, of the Poldice Valley Trust, rang me one day to ask if I would consider writing a small book or perhaps just a few leaflets detailing walks and rides for cyclists and horse-riders in and around the Valley, together with some background information, I was attracted to the idea. By then I had also completed *A View from Carn Brea*, which along with the first volume covered a large proportion of the Mineral Tramways route across Cornwall, as described by the Cornwall Archaeological Unit's report on the Mineral Tramways Project (1990). One very important section of that route was omitted from both my books, however: the inland end of the Portreath Tramway, south of what is now the A30, and the branch of the Redruth and Chasewater Railway which started at Hale Mills near Twelveheads and ran into the Poldice Valley, stopping only a few hundred yards short of the Portreath Tramway terminus. Chris's invitation provided the golden opportunity to complete the picture, so I decided to accept.

What I had not bargained for was the discovery of so much beauty. As I have said, I knew the area was historically interesting and indeed important, but my vague general impression of the twin valleys (Poldice and Wheal Maid) was that of a barren industrial wasteland. When I started to explore the area I was amazed by the rich variety of plant and animal life inhabiting it, and by its colourfulness: mine-shaft openings choked with flowers, shrubs and even trees; breathtaking expanses of gorse and heather alive with bees; garden plants such as roses and cotoneasters, perhaps there as proof that even fly-tipping can have a silver lining. The very minerals for which this landscape was exploited over so many centuries make a startling contribution to its special palette of colours. For the first time in writing a book of walks in Cornwall I became convinced that a section of colour photographs was essential.

Among the many delights of wandering around Poldice is the sense that you are free to roam wherever your fancy dictates. By and large in practice this is true, but please bear in mind that all the land is owned by private individuals, companies or local authorities, and that many of the inviting tracks and paths are not official rights of way. I have tried to ensure that all the walks and rides recommended in this book keep to routes which are rights of way, either in law or at least by virtue of long-established custom, but I must stress that the inclusion of any path, track or road in my directions cannot in itself give you the right to use it. Ultimately, the responsibility for where you go must be your own; and in saying that I am thinking also of the dangers inherent in exploring old mining regions.

Although my own name is on the cover as the author of this book, in fact a lot of it was contributed by Chris Massie. In particular, the sections on geological history, steam engines and the Williams – Taylor rivalry are based closely on material he provided. I am also indebted to Eric Rabjohns and Bernadette Fallon, who read through much of the typescript and made many useful suggestions and corrections, and to Bryan Earl, author of *Cornish Mining*, for the information he gave me on arsenic production and the designs of buddles.

Bob Acton

4

SHORT STROLLS AROUND THE POLDICE VALLEY

The area once mined by Poldice and Wheal Unity is a maze of tracks, paths and roads, old and new. The map on the centre pages shows the main ones. The circled numbers on that map, 1-8, indicate points of interest described in the following notes, and I have put them in an order which would enable you to visit them all on one "round walk". Alternatively, of course, you could devise your own routes to take in just the ones you wish. See page 2 for a note about parking.

1.   *WHEAL UNITY*

Although there is so little of this mine to see on the surface now (just a few low walls remaining of an engine house, plus shafts and waste-tips or "burrows"), it was once one of the richest in the area. There may well have been small mines here in earlier times, but Wheal Unity itself seems, according to H.G.Dines in his authoritative *The Metalliferous Mining Region of South-West England* (1956), to have started about 1790, although Hamilton Jenkin in *The Cornish Miner* writes, "In 1773 the women breaking ores by hand at Wheal Unity .... were getting 5d a day." Already by 1798 it had made profits of over £100,000, mainly from sales of copper ore. Soon after that it was amalgamated with Poldice Mine, but its accounts continued to be recorded separately, so we know that it went on doing well: D.B.Barton claims that by 1818 it "had for some years been the principal copper mine in Cornwall, other than Dolcoath and the United Mines and, even though it declined after a peak output of almost 7,000 tons in 1816, it was still the most important mine around St Day." (*Essays in Cornish Mining History*, Vol. 2, 1970) J.H.Collins (1912) says that its total profits amounted to £400,000. By the middle of the 19th century it was dependent on selling arsenic, along with a little tin. Surprisingly, Dines refers to Unity as a tin mine, and gives no hint that it ever produced copper. In 1864 it became part of St Day United Mines.

Ruined engine house, Wheal Unity

Like its neighbour Wheal Gorland (see Walk 1), Unity was famous for producing rare and beautiful mineral specimens such as chalcophyllite, olivenite ("wood copper") and mimetite. Examples of each, all from Unity, are shown in *Minerals of Cornwall and Devon* by P.G.Embrey and R.F.Symes (1987): see pages 94–5 and 115. Gorland, Unity and Wheal Muttrell (which became part of Gorland) were known particularly for producing "classic" specimens of the lovely blue crystals called liroconite (page 113). James King, of County Maps and Minerals in Truro, tells me that the miners were well aware of the value of such specimens, and would smuggle them out of the mine by covering them with a type of soft white clay found underground. Sometimes they enlisted the help of bal maidens, who could secrete the minerals among their voluminous skirts.

Wheal Unity's dressing floors, where the ore was crushed and prepared for smelting, were a little way to the west, at or close to Little Beside. The dressing processes required a constant and copious supply of water, and it was decided that the best source for this was the adit of Pednandrea Mine, Redruth – a surprising decision, because it entailed the construction of a leat six miles long, including over four thousand feet of tunnel. Richard Thomas's Geological Map of 1819 clearly shows the leat, starting at Plain-An-Gwarry, on the north side of Redruth. It snakes its way northwards, following the contour line through Gilbert's Coombe and North Country, then still further north to Kerrow Farm, not far south of Mawla. There it turns south-east, running roughly parallel with the Portreath tramway and entering the tunnel just south of Wheal Rose. Next it passes under what are now the A30 and the main railway line, and surfaces close to the St Day-Scorrier road, roughly where the drive to Killifreth Farm begins. For the last mile-or-so it runs along the western side of the tramway, apparently coming to an end at the St Day-Chacewater road, at the point where the Unity Fuse Works was later built. This is just one example among many of the ingenuity and determined effort devoted by Cornish mining engineers to the harnessing of water power. For another, see the note on Paynter's Pool; and for the most spectacular of all, explore the Luxulyan Valley. (See *Around the River Fowey*, Walk 12.)

2.   **MINE SHAFTS**
The Poldice valley is riddled with mine shafts. H.G.Dines lists at least twenty for Poldice Mine alone, and each has a name, usually the surname of a mine official responsible for sinking it, or perhaps of an "adventurer" (shareholder) who helped finance the work – though "Kitty Billy's Shaft" seems unlikely to fit either of those categories. Dines also gives the depths of the shafts: Richards', for example (not the deepest), descended to 153 fathoms below adit, that is, 918 feet below the drainage shaft, which was itself 288 feet down. The physical labour involved, first in digging such a shaft and hauling out the waste material, and later in descending and climbing the ladders before and after a hard day's work, often in hot and stifling conditions, requires a strong effort of the imagination to grasp. When a mine, or perhaps one or two sections of it, closed down, abandoned shafts were often left open as traps for the unwary, or boarded over a few feet down. Rubble and soil would be heaped over the boards and the shaft would be forgotten .... until the boards rotted away and provided a nasty shock for an unsuspecting cottager or farmer. The mouths of many shafts have become choked by the collapse of the stone or brick "collars" that were built round the top few feet, or by the dumping of

rubbish in them: these types are obviously particularly dangerous, and you should never ignore the triangular warning signs erected in recent years. Some of the old shafts at Poldice are surrounded by fences or walls; others are capped with solid concrete platforms – safer and perhaps less unsightly, but leaving no access to the shafts for bats and other creatures who have colonised them, and preventing ventilation of the mine workings. During the last ten years, the conical metal cages called Clwyd Caps have been much used, but these are condemned by the Cornwall Archaeological Unit as giving "the appearance of security without actually guaranteeing it in the long term" (Mineral Tramways Project report, 1990); the Unit favours "anchored steel-reinforced concrete rafts" where capping is necessary, and walling or barbed-wire fencing elsewhere. Todpool Shaft of Wheal Unity, marked 2 on the map, remains as it was left when the mine closed, except that it is now surrounded by thick vegetation including a sycamore hanging perilously over the chasm. The shrubs, gorse, heather and other flora here are particularly beautiful in late summer: see colour photograph 3.

Arsenic condensing chambers, Poldice

3.   ***POLDICE MINE AND ARSENIC WORKS***
(Colour photographs 1 and 2.)

In 1512 during a court hearing at Exeter, one witness mentioned the theft of some tin near "Poldyth in Wennap". In 1678, another court case arose from a dispute about the supply of water to the stamps at Poldice; the matter was still not settled when in 1681 Poldice was described as "an ancient tin work which hath produced great advantage to his most Sacred Majestie, some years above £1200 per annum..." Four years later, William Hals wrote: "Not far from this place (St Day) is that unparalleled and inexhaustible tin work called Poldys (the top or head of Dysstown) which for about forty years space hath employed yearly from eight hundred to a thousand men and boys labouring for and searching after tin in that place where they have produced and raised up for that time yearly, at least £20,000 worth of that commodity to the great enrichment of the soil, of the bound owner, and of adventurers in these lands." Hals' explanation of the name Poldice is open to question: the 18th century historian Thomas Tonkin wrote that "the right name of this famous work, which is esteemed to be the deepest in the county, being 106 fms., is Pul Dye's, St Dye's Pits or Mines"; and according to C.C.James *dice* has nothing to do with St Day but refers to ricks. An account from the 1720s mentions "engines" for pumping out the water there, but the machinery in use then would have had a hard struggle to cope with water at such depths (over 600 feet). The problem was alleviated by the building of the great County Adit, begun in 1748 (see Walk 4), but 30 years later the Newcomen engines were still having difficulty in raising the water as far as the adit. In the 1780s, four of the new Boulton & Watt engines replaced them, and these apparently proved adequate. It was only at about this time that copper began to be more important than tin at Poldice, and although it produced a very large amount of copper during the next hundred years, as a copper mine it never quite recaptured the pre-eminence it once had. Even so, it was among the earliest mines to employ one of the huge 90" Woolf engines, made in Wales. It was erected at Bissa Pool Shaft in 1821. In the *West Briton* on 16 November it was reported that because of bad weather "the whole of this immense engine .... which weighs about 15 tons was landed at the Port of Padstow" (rather than Hayle), "a distance of some thirty miles from the mine, only 29 days before it was set at work - the nozzels and many other parts of it were at that time in Wales." Only two other engines of equal size and power were at work anywhere in the world, and they had both been erected nearby at Consols within the preceding year. After 1852, when Poldice became part of St Day United, its output is not recorded separately, but by 1860 the Cornish copper industry was clearly in decline, and D.B.Barton includes St Day United in his list of mines which closed between 1866 and 1868. In 1870, it seems, a new start was made by the group under the name of Poldice Mines. Barton refers to "the closing of Poldice in June 1873", but the reference books quote figures for output of copper, tin and other metals up to 1893. Hardly anything remains of the many large engine houses: here and there beside old shafts are small groups of shaped granite blocks or bricks, and most of a bob wall (the thick wall which supported the beam of a Cornish engine) overhangs Engine Shaft, marked on the plan at the centre of the book.

According to some historians including D.B.Barton and Bryan Earl (though Roger Burt has cast doubts on this view), one factor which delayed final closure for many Cornish mines was the sudden increase in demand for arsenic during the early 1870s, when its value as an insecticide began to be realised, especially in controlling Colorado beetles on potato plants. Its use for several other purposes was already known; these included sheep dips, soap for cleaning leather, the clarification of glass, a process in the manufacture of lead shot, and pigments, particularly a brilliant green much used in Victorian wallpapers which became notorious when acidic pollution in city air reacted with it to produce deadly arsene gas. Nearby mines such as Killifreth and Great Wheal Busy set up plants for arsenic production, and although the arsenic trade declined during the 1880s there were revivals later, for example in 1906, during World War I, and again in 1923-4. (Bryan Earl states that the need for arsenic in the manufacture of poison gas during the First World War caused its price to rise from £9 a ton to over £100; after 1918 the pre-war prices returned.) All the obvious buildings remaining at Poldice Mine are relics of an arsenic works; the oldest parts of it date from the 1870s, but there were many additions and modifications over the 50-or-so years of its active existence. The basic process for obtaining the arsenic was simple. The first small arsenic works in Britain was set up a short way south of Poldice, at Perranarworthal, in 1812; until then, the arsenic in the ore was usually regarded merely as a nuisance, and was driven off by roasting the ore in a "calciner" (pronounced "cal-<u>sign</u>-er") or "burning house"; during the 1830s an improved type of calciner invented by William Brunton was introduced

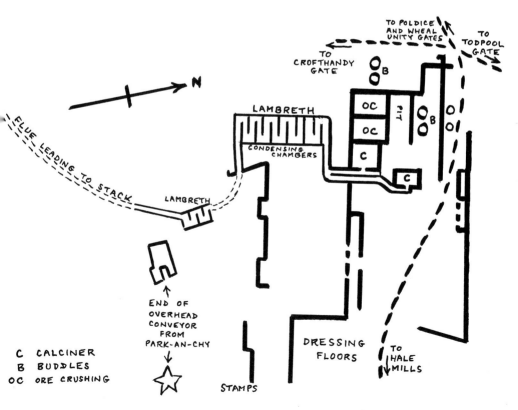

C   CALCINER
B   BUDDLES
OC ORE CRUSHING

which rotated automatically, ensuring that the ore was roasted evenly. This was a very efficient design: some Brunton calciners, according to Bryan Earl, "served continuously for a hundred years." "In such a calciner, at South Crofty," he writes, "seen working in 1950, the fires burnt away merrily and there was surprisingly no smell of arsenic – nor did anyone seem at all concerned about the thoroughly deadly gas streaming away in the hot flue .... There was a decidedly '18th century' atmosphere about the whole operation of grimy individuals amongst glowing fires at the side of cramped and dusty stone passages." (*Journal of the Trevithick Society* No. 10, 1983) Quite well preserved Brunton calciners can be seen at Great Wheal Busy (Walk 2), and there is an almost complete one in the Tolgus Valley, on the left just beyond the A30 viaduct as you drive from Redruth to Portreath. To collect the arsenic, all that had to be added was a long flue including at least one zizgag section (called a lambreth, presumably a Cornish version of labyrinth) with a tall stack at the far end to create a strong through-draught and also to reduce the damage caused by the noxious fumes that issued from it. As the gas cooled in the lambreth, the arsenic condensed and formed crystals on the walls. When sufficient had collected, the calciners were stopped, iron doors in the lambreth were opened, and the arsenic "soot" was swept and shovelled out. Finally this was taken to a refinery – probably Conn's chemical works at Point Mills or Todd's Arsenic and Paint Works, Bissoe, in the case of Poldice – to be roasted in furnaces like those used for smelting tin, linked to further condensing chambers, and ground into powder ready for sale. As well as arsenic, sulphur was obtained as a result of the refining process; some of that was used to manufacture sulphuric acid, and there were at least two vitriol works in the Bissoe Valley: Paynter's, near Bissoe Bridge, and another a little way beyond the viaduct. Precautions to protect the arsenic workers were only rudimentary – wads of cotton wool in the nostrils and a cloth over the mouth, together with strict regulations about washing. Skin rashes and sores were common, especially in warm weather when the men sweated. In general, though, they seem to have remained surprisingly healthy, perhaps because they developed an immunity to the poison; it was even claimed that the arsenic promoted plump skin, a good complexion and thick, shiny hair. Three excellent photographs of the arsenic refinery at Roseworthy, north-west of Camborne, are included in J.H.Trounson's *Mining in Cornwall*, Vol. 2 (Nos. 54-6). At Poldice there were two calciners, one of which is dated 1883. Notice how in at least two places within the group of buildings the flue is raised above head height to pass over an archway. As you explore these remains you may notice the characteristic smell of arsenic, which I have seen described as "like stale cooked onions."

The last chapter in the story of Poldice's part in Cornish mining history concerns another mine, Park-an-Chy, about a mile to the north-west. This was re-opened several times near the start of this century for the production of tin and wolfram, a mineral valued mainly for its use in tungsten lamp filaments. Water supplies for dressing the ore at Park-an-Chy were inadequate, so between 1926 and 1929 the ore was transported to Poldice by means of overhead cables passing through St Day: see Walk 1, section 9. Parts of the concrete structures which formed the terminus of this system can still be seen at Poldice, beside the dressing floors south and east of the arsenic works. Recovering both the tin and the wolfram was very difficult, because fine crushing was necessary for the former and coarse for the latter.

4.   **BUDDLES**

At least three pairs of round buddles survive beside the Poldice arsenic works ruins, each pair consisting of one convex and one concave. The stone bases of the two pairs shown on the plan of the site are well preserved, but of course their wooden superstructures have gone. Buddles were used for separating the valuable, metal-bearing grains of crushed ore from waste material or "gangue". The earliest type of buddle was rectangular. The rather quaint definition of "buddles" by C.C.James in his *History of the Parish of Gwennap* is, "Pits, 7 feet long and 3 feet wide and 2½ feet deep, dug near a stamping mill. Stamped tin is curiously washed from its impurities by water constantly running through the buddles, while a boy is standing in it working with a shovel and also with his feet." Round buddles, developed in Wales, eventually superseded the rectangular ones. The "pulp" from the stamps (see note 6) was fed to the centre of a convex buddle and agitated by rotating brushes so that the heavier grains settled near the centre and the lighter were washed down to the edges. Commonly, the metal-bearing "slimes" from the convex buddle were next fed to the outer edge of a concave one. Bryan Earl's *Cornish Mining*, pages 83-5, has explanations of the various types of buddle and the "round frame", a more sophisticated version of the concave buddle which began to be used in Cornwall in the 1870s; my sketches may help to give you some idea of what they looked like when working. The waste matter ("tailings") from the buddles and round frames still contained fine particles of metal, and some of these were recovered by passing the slimes over wooden "tables", tipped by hand. By the end of the century, the larger mines were using devices such as Frue Vanners which vibrated the tables automatically. These were labour-saving and more efficient, but even they failed to extract all the metal, and as ever-better methods of separation have been developed, much of the gangue from earlier times has been re-processed. (An excellent way to gain some practical understanding of these matters is to visit the Tolgus Tin-Streaming Works at the National Gold Centre on the Redruth-Portreath road.)

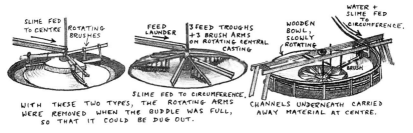

WITH THESE TWO TYPES, THE ROTATING ARMS WERE REMOVED WHEN THE BUDDLE WAS FULL, SO THAT IT COULD BE DUG OUT.

CHANNELS UNDERNEATH CARRIED AWAY MATERIAL AT CENTRE.

CONVEX AND CONCAVE BUDDLES   ROUND FRAME

5.   ***PAYNTER'S POOL***

This was dug in order to store water for use on the dressing floors of Poldice Mine: the small stone wall at the east end of the pool may mark the original position of a sluice gate, and from there you can still trace the first part of the curving channel by which water was fed down to the mine.   As mentioned on page 51, the spring called Vogue Shoot, beside the road to Gwennap Pit near the Star Inn, provided domestic water supplies for St Day, and at Five Shoots near Tolcarne some of the water that remained was tapped for Paynter's Pool.   It got there by means of a long leat and wooden launders passing through Tressadern farmyard and along Trewelm Lane, Crofthandy.   Until the 1960s, this system was kept in good order, because the pool was used by livestock (as well as providing a bathing pool for local youngsters), but when mains water arrived the leat fell into disrepair and the pool dried up.   The *Poldice Bugle* of September 1990 reported that a start had been made on a scheme to refill the pool using water drained from a nearby hill.   (The track beside the pool, by the way, was once a short tramway to the Crofthandy coal yard at the terminus of the Portreath Tramway.)

The stamps engine house at Killifreth Mine, with 64 heads of stamps
(Photograph reproduced by courtesy of the Royal Institution of Cornwall)

6.   ***CORNISH AND CALIFORNIAN STAMPS***
                  AND OTHER ORE-CRUSHING MACHINERY

The large lumps of ore brought up from the mines were – until stone-breaking machinery was introduced, late last century – first broken into small pieces (normally about two inches) "by hand", that is, by hammers wielded usually by the women known as "bal maidens" (mine girls).   The pieces, mixed with water, were fed to a crushing machine which reduced them to sand-like particles.   The resulting "slimes" were passed through copper sieves and gravity methods were then used to separate the heavier, metal-bearing particles from the rest: see the earlier note on buddles. Many ore-crushing machines were made by Harvey & Co. at their Hayle foundry, and Harvey's 1884 catalogue, republished by Bradford Barton and still available in bookshops, includes clear engravings and explanations of the main types. Cornish Stamps in their most rudimentary form were already in use by Tudor times: Richard Carew's *Survey of Cornwall* (1602) mentions "a stamping mill, where three, and in some places sixe great logges of timber, bound at the ends with yron, and lifted up and down by a wheel, driven with the water, doe break it smaller." Similar machines had been employed at mines in Germany even earlier: a drawing of one was published by Agricola in 1556 and is reproduced by Dr R.L.Atkinson in her *Tin and Tin Mining* (Shire Publications, 1985). In later versions, the "logges" were replaced by iron "heads" weighing from 3 to 6 cwt, and the larger batteries of stamps – some of them with as many as 120 heads – were worked by steam engines. Californian Stamps began to be used in Cornwall in 1857; in Harvey's catalogue they are called "Special Revolving Ore Stamps", referring to the fact that the heads rotated and therefore wore much more evenly. They were also much faster than Cornish Stamps. A complete set of Californian Stamps can be seen at King Edward Mine, near Troon: see Walk 12 in my *A View from Carn Brea*. Further improvements followed, such as the "Oscillating Cylinder Stamps" illustrated on page 31 of the catalogue; and for breaking copper ore there were crushing rollers: page 39. For many decades – especially between about 1750 and 1850, and again for several periods up to 1929 – the Poldice valley must have echoed to the ear-splitting noise from these machines. The strong foundations ("plats") that had to be built for the largest batteries of stamps and rollers can still be seen in several places, notably beside Bissa Pool and on the slope above, at the point where the mineral railway branch seems to have come to an end, and also beside the dressing floors at Poldice itself.

7.   *BISSA POOL*
Before the County Adit was driven, in the middle of the 18th century, many of the mines it served drained into the Poldice valley, providing an energy source for numerous waterwheels. It seems that the valley was dammed at this point to create a reservoir for supplying the wheels in periods of drought, and perhaps also as a drinking-place for stock. As with Paynter's Pool, the Poldice Valley Trust hopes before long to be able to re-fill Bissa Pool, whose name, "pool of the birch trees", is a reminder of the pretty, rural spot which this valley must once have been. For a note about the County Adit, see Walk 4.

8.   *MINE WASTE DUMPS*
Perhaps the most noticeable dumps in the valley – apart from the new tip on the upper slopes of the Goongumpas side – are the whitish heaps just east of the arsenic works. Known locally as "The Sands", these are a legacy of the period (1926-9) when material from Park-an-Chy was processed here: see the note on Poldice. In fact, of course, the valley is a happy hunting ground for collectors of minerals, because unwanted material brought to the surface by mining operations is scattered everywhere, much of it still in the form of spoil heaps (known in Cornwall as burrows); in particular, stone excavated during the sinking of shafts is often piled around their mouths. An old burrow which has been left

undisturbed can be a valuable source of information about the mine, its methods, and the geology of the "sett" it was working; but the Poldice valley was a busy centre of industrial activity for centuries, and probably most of the dumps have been shifted around, or added to at various times from various sources, or reprocessed for the minerals still in them, or quarried for hardcore and other building materials. Such disturbances of the dumps tend to bring toxic minerals to the surface, inhibiting plant-growth and creating the sort of moon-landscape to be seen especially around the Consols workings in the southern valley; but when they are left untouched most of them are colonised by heather, gorse and other plants including escapes from gardens, and they become (as the Mineral Tramways Project report puts it) "rare and unusual habitats" as well as areas with a special beauty of their own.

Treatment of waste tips above Bissa Pool at Poldice, about 1924-9. Steam power was used throughout. The map on the centre pages indicates roughly where this photograph was taken. (Reproduced by courtesy of the Royal Institution of Cornwall)

SECTION 2

TWO MEDIUM—LENGTH WALKS

The route of Walk A is shown on the large-scale map at the centre of the book, and that of Walk B on the map for Walk 3 (page 33). Fuller details about points of interest are given in Sections 1 and 3. For a note about parking see page 2.

A   "THE GOONGUMPAS LOOP"

Nearly 2½ miles.

"Goongumpas" (sometimes spelt Goongumpus) means "level downland", and this delightful little walk matches that description: there's little climbing to do, but you are on a hill which is a green haven between the two highly industrialised valleys and provides good views of both.

From Wheal Unity Gate, walk to Crofthandy Gate and take the track beside Paynter's Pool. At the fork go right, and when you reach the track leading to Goongumpas Gate, turn right on that. About 20 yards before the Poldice Valley sign, walk up on the left beside a hedge, on the right-hand edge of Douce Coppice (named after the firm with a licence to tip nearby: they sponsored the tree-planting here). This path – sometimes rather overgrown towards the top – brings you to another track. Turn left on that. At the house on the left, Goonhillend Cottage, a modern menhir has been erected in the garden – called The Goonstone, according to Chris Massie. John Layte, who lives at the cottage, tells me it is not a quarried block but a naturally weathered moorstone from the Lizard peninsula. (Compare "The Menhirs" at Hale Mills Farm ..... and of course "The Stones", near Padstow, a modern bungalow whose small garden rivals Stonehenge, Men-an-Tol and Logan Rock combined.) The track soon becomes a "green lane", and then quite a narrow path which might sometimes be overgrown, though it was perfectly walkable in September 1990. The wide view includes the ivy-covered stack and engine house of Wheal Henry to the left, those of Wheal Fortune right, and Carnon Downs in the far distance ahead. The path curves right and joins another one. Here, turning left would bring you down to Hale Mills; but to complete the "loop" go right. The attractiveness of this path, with its good views over the southern valley and beyond, is somewhat threatened in one place by a thick growth of Japanese Knotweed, a plant which rivals the wild rhododendron for invasiveness and indestructibility. As the path widens to a track, St Day Church appears, straight ahead, and up on the right are the old buildings of Goon Farm – possibly once a mine's Count House (offices). The wind pump used once to raise water from the nearby mineshaft for domestic and farm supply. Soon on the left there are good views of Mount Wellington's tailings dam; then you are among houses at Lower Goongumpas Lane. At the Chapel turn right past Crofthandy Gate along Higher Goongumpas Lane and take the left-hand track to return to Wheal Unity Gate.

B WHEAL UNITY TO HALE MILLS AND BACK

Nearly 3 miles.

This is an interesting round walk which takes in many of the main points described elsewhere. One possible route keeps to the Poldice valley; two other choices are also given, involving the southern valley and Goongumpas.

Start as for Walk 3, but instead of turning left up the path (start of point 2, page 34), keep to the lowest track, following the line of granite parish boundary markers. On the right near the one numbered 57 are what look like the ruins of an engine house. Numbers 70-74 are at Hale Mills, where the valleys meet, and the stream from the southern one - a mere trickle in September 1990 - gives an ochre stain to the valley bottom from here on. Follow the grassy path on the left for a few yards further, watching for stone number 76. Beside it a small path goes left, and if you can get through the brambles and nettles you will see that it leads to an old wooden gate beyond which is a cleft in the rocks - probably a natural fissure but apparently used as a mine adit. Chris Massie tells me that the small enclosures and sheds nearby used to be owned by a Mr Archie Jewell; he had a cottage here, and his water supply was this well or adit - hence the alkathene pipe. Chris calls the path along here the Jewell Carriageway. Before long it descends to the valley bottom, crosses the stream bed and joins the main track from Twelveheads. Here turn sharp right, back to Hale Mills. The bell-turret which makes an outbuilding look like an old school is one of several jokes at the entrance to Hale Mills Farm: notice the "menhirs", and the "gate posts" made from giant iron pipes. Perhaps the millstone is a genuine relic of one of the Hale (otherwise known as Middle) Mills. According to A.H.Unwin, "the Hale Mills were converted from tin-stamping to corn-grinding" in about 1922 (*Journal of the Trevithick Society* No. 14, 1987). ("Hayle" and "Hail" are spellings seen on some maps. It probably derives from the Cornish *hal*, a moor or marsh.)

Here are three possible routes back to Wheal Unity:

For Nos. 1 and 2, go left past the old miners' cottages, through the tunnel under the railway embankment, up the zigzag path on the right to the top of the dam wall, and then either (1) go straight on along the main track beside the tailings reservoir, over the stile at the end, and back to Wheal Unity via Lower Goongumpas Lane and Crofthandy Gate; or (2) continue zigzagging up, passing left of two mineshafts with "Clwyd caps", and go left at the top. You are now on the second half of the "Goongumpas Loop".

For No. 3, go right at Hale Mills and keep to the left side of the Poldice valley using the higher track, which gives you a different perspective, offering for example a better view of the ivy-covered stack (Wheal Henry) and various shafts or small quarries on the far side, along with ruined engine houses, stamps foundations and other old mine buildings beside the track you are on. When the arsenic works buildings at Poldice come into view, head for them: there's a maze of tracks and paths, but you can't go far wrong. After passing among the buildings, use the Poldice Valley map at the centre of the book if necessary to guide you back to Wheal Unity Gate.

1. The ruined flue and stack of Poldice arsenic works

2. Poldice arsenic works
OPPOSITE (Above) 3. Todpool Shaft, Wheal Unity
*   (Below) 4. The tailings dam with the Consols clock tower and engine houses*

5. The ochre-stained stream at Hale Mills, with the railway embankment behind

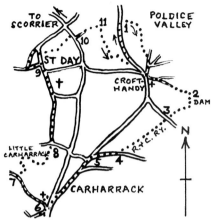

NO. 1 : CARHARRACK AND ST DAY
A little over 3 miles.

After crossing the southern valley, giving a good view of the work carried out to provide a tailings dam for Mount Wellington Mine, this walk follows the course of the Redruth and Chasewater Railway across farmland and through the centre of the old mining village of Carharrack. It then turns north, along tracks and minor roads, to St Day, still interesting and attractive despite the fact that its heyday as the hub of the world's most important copper-mining district has long gone. After a brief tour of some of the most historic parts of the town, the walk returns to the starting point via tracks, one of which follows the route of the Poldice Tramway into Crofthandy. The walk avoids roads almost completely, except in Carharrack and St Day. You will find shops and toilets in both, and each has a friendly, unpretentious pub that serves good food: both of them are "locals" in the best sense. The St Day Inn is particularly attractive: "a hub of village life," comments David Guthrie in Cornish Pubs. "Vestige of a rapidly disappearing breed."

1 From Wheal Unity Gate, take the track ahead towards the ruined chimney at first. Keep right where the main track forks, and just after that fork right again. This track brings you to Crofthandy Gate. Continue ahead along Higher Goongumpas Lane, and at Crofthandy (✱) Methodist Church turn left along Lower Goongumpas Lane. Ignore the left fork and continue straight on till you reach a stile set in a high mesh fence.

2 Go over the stile and then turn right to cross the valley. If you walk on the dam embankment you will have a good view of the tailings dam (✱); on the far side, turn right on the track, and fork right (on the lower track),

---

CROFTHANDY
Oliver Padel says the name derives from croft, 'uncultivated, enclosed land' (land, according to Charles Henderson, on which gorse was grown high for fuel), plus perhaps hensy, 'ancient house, ruins, remains'; Padel offers no suggestion as to what ruins might be meant. C.C.James suggested the name means "Hendy's croft", and thought Crofthandy "was probably a centre for smuggled goods. Old inhabitants formerly spoke of 'headless horses having been seen in the neighbourhood.' The smugglers no doubt encouraged the publication of the story as a stratagem to encourage the villagers to stay indoors when the goods were arriving." Just when this took place, he doesn't say; at first sight, Crofthandy seems an unlikely haven for contraband. Was it brought from Portreath to the depot at the end of the tramway?

TAILINGS DAM *(Colour photograph 4.)*

In a modern metal mine, when all the valuable minerals have, as far as possible, been recovered, water containing the fine waste particles is piped into a reservoir. There they gradually sink to the bottom, and the water is returned to the mine for re-use. Eventually, when the tailings filled the reservoir and dried out, the area would in theory be landscaped and grassed over; in practice, however, some tin still remains, and with improved technology the tailings may be re-worked if tin prices justify it. This dam was constructed not just for Mount Wellington Mine but also as part of Billaton Minerals' ambitious scheme (early 1980s) for recovering alluvial tin by dredging Restronguet Creek.

---

passing through an open area scarred by recent industry. Alternatively you could cross the valley on the track below the embankment, which gives you a good view of the way the stream is led by a conduit under the floor of the planned reservoir; it emerges at Hale Mills. Follow the path to the right, beside a fence, on the far side, which brings you to the open area just mentioned. On the far side of that, take the upper track ahead, the trackbed of the Redruth and Chasewater Railway (*). This soon reaches a road.

3 Cross that and continue opposite along the trackbed, now a path between wire fences. After about 100 yards, barbed wire crosses the path, but it is easy to duck under. (A stile is needed here, and will perhaps have materialised by the time you do this walk.) Continue in the same line, beside the hedge on your right. The ruined building ahead is the remains of the railway's Great Yard (colour photograph 9), built about 1851 to house an office and eight storage bays for coal and other goods. At this point there was a branch line east to Ale and Cakes (part of United Mines), and from that line another branch went back, parallel with the main line but on a higher level, through Wheal Virgin to Wheal Fortune (both parts of Consols). The way ahead is barred by a wall; if you are agile you could climb over it, but it's easier and more interesting to walk through the Great Yard. When you emerge from it, continue ahead with the hedge on your left – still the course of the railway – and go through the farm gate on to Consols Road.

4 Walk along the road, still in roughly the same direction. The new bungalows on the left have obliterated the railway track, but its course through the centre of Carharrack can quite easily be traced. Perhaps you would enjoy doing your own detective work, so in the next few lines I'll limit myself to just a couple of references to the railway; turn to page 27 for a detailed account of its route through the village. At the road junction continue ahead along Fore Street (not named at this end) into Carharrack (*), passing the Mills' Hall (*), the playing field where the public toilets are, and the Seven Stars.

5 At the main road you need to go a few yards to the right to see remains of the railway; but for the main walk route, turn left past the shops then first right (Chapel Terrace), then left again in front of the Methodist Church (note its date, just when the boom in copper mining would have been causing rapid growth in village population) and along the short path that brings you to Wheal Damsel Road. The house on the corner opposite

THE REDRUTH AND CHASEWATER RAILWAY
(Colour photographs 7, 8 and 9.)

The Redruth and Chasewater was Cornwall's first true railway, in the sense of employing wagons with flanged wheels, unlike the Poldice Tramway (see Walk 2). When mines in the southern part of Gwennap parish, such as Consols, began to be very productive, in the early 1820s, an efficient link with a south coast port became increasingly necessary, for the export of copper ore to South Wales for smelting (Cornwall having no coal deposits), and the import of coal. (During one year in the 1830s, Consols and United Mines alone consumed 15,000 tons of coal.) As early as 1808, a plan had been put forward for a canal from Bissoe to Devoran, but the success of the tramway linking Poldice and Portreath during the next decade pointed the way to a better solution. In 1819, the Norwich-born businessman John Taylor (1779-1863) acquired the lease of the group of old mines known as Consols, and in 1824 his London-based company received Royal Assent to an Act of Parliament permitting the building of what was then called "The Redruth Railway". The new line was officially opened in January 1826, and by 1827 it extended from Pednandrea Mine, Redruth, to Point, a mile beyond Devoran on Restronguet Creek. A branch line through Twelveheads to Chacewater was planned but never built. Horses drew the wagons until steam locomotives were introduced in 1854, except on the section below Devoran. At first there were two engines, called Miner and Smelter; a third, Spitfire, was added in 1859, by which time the line was handling 90,000 tons of freight per year. The railway closed in 1915, but most of its course can still be traced. More details are in the notes on Walk 5 of *A View from Carn Marth*, and some discussion of the history of the proposed branch line from Hale Mills to Wheal Busy via Poldice will be found on page 70. For a full treatment of the subject, see D.B.Barton's *The Redruth and Chasewater Railway* (1960). Many people are puzzled by the spelling, "Chasewater". I have heard it said that this was simply a mistake on the part of an official in London, but Barton's explanation is that it is "a legacy of the days of its (the Railway's) formation when this was the more customary spelling." Certainly Richard Thomas consistently used it in his *Report on a Survey of the Mining District from Chasewater to Camborne* (1819).

was once a pub, The Steam Engine; see the drawing on page 19 of *A View from Carn Marth*, also available as a postcard in Carharrack Post Office. Cross to that and continue ahead for some 200 yards to see the original footbridge over the line, recently restored by Carharrack Parish Council (not by the Trevithick Society as stated in the above book). Granite setts from the old railway are plentiful around here, built into garden walls, for example, and forming some of the steps up to the bridge.

6 Return to Wheal Damsel (*) Road and turn up it.

7 After about a quarter of a mile, several tracks converge at an open space on the right. Take the one passing just to the left of the cottages, which soon curves downhill towards St Day. At the broken Public Bridleway sign, turn right past the house called Northwethel, passing among other houses. This is Little Carharrack. The Manor House is very old, and C.C.James suggests that it may have been a lodging-house for pilgrims travelling between the shrines of St Day and St Michael's Mount. Next go left and follow the Public Footpath sign.

CARHARRACK

The name is locally pronounced "C'rarrick". Padel suggests that it means "fort of the high place". I have not come across an explanation of which fort or high place may have been referred to, but of course Carn Marth is very close, and it would be surprising if that has never been fortified. The setting of the village must once have looked very different: even now there is woodland close by to the south, and there is evidence to suggest that oak woods once covered much if not all of Carn Marth, as with the neighbouring Carn Brea. C.C.James says there were just twelve cottages at Carharrack in 1770, but the boom in copper mining caused rapid growth, and this was accelerated by the coming of the railway. "The railway," writes D.B.Barton, "was very much part and parcel of Carharrack's daily life. For years many of the railway horses were stabled there and almost all the working population of the village was employed in Consols, United or the other copper mines nearby." One of those, not mentioned elsewhere in this book, was Ting Tang Mine, on the railway's route between here and Lanner. In recent years, much interesting material about Carharrack has been gathered by local historians, notably Barrie May and Eric Rabjohns; their exhibition was on display at the Methodist Church for the second time in 1990, and if it is given further airings I'd strongly recommend a visit.

MILLS' HALL

William John Mills, from St Day, was a successful businessman who devoted much of his wealth to local charity and other good causes, notably in 1933 by buying a complete street in St Day and converting it as free housing for elderly people. Elsewhere in the locality he provided public playing-fields and gardens, and a Village Hall for Carharrack. As you will see, this is the headquarters of the local brass band; the words "and St Day" were added to its name in return for financial help from the Mills family.

WHEAL DAMSEL

C.C.James and J.H.Collins both call this copper-producer a "very ancient mine," and James says that in 1806 it "was the richest in the parish (Gwennap), and possibly in the county." Its surface buildings must, I think, have been at or near the point where three tracks meet the road, as mentioned in the directions. In 1818 it was employing 240 people, and the deepest workings were about a thousand feet below surface. The last figures for production I have come across are from 1872, but it may have continued beyond that date. Incidentally, many Cornish mines bear feminine names (Jane, Frances and Kitty, for example); often these refer to the wife or daughter of the mine owner or some other official. Wheal Damsel was once linked with another mine called Wheal Spinster, both worked the same lode as Wheal Maid or Maiden and Wheal Virgin, further east, and Wheal Girl was close to those; it would be interesting to know if the same lady is alluded to in all these names, and if so, who she was.

8 Cross the road, go through the gap in the wooden fencing and up the fairly steep road ahead into St Day (*), passing the school. Continue ahead at the road junction, past the ruins of the "old" church. The new one, on the opposite side of the road, has an interesting collection of photographs of St Day dating from about 1910; if the room containing them is locked, you may be able to get in by contacting Father Paul Foot at the vicarage nearby. Go on along Church Street, past some shops.

9 Turn left at Fore Street (signed Redruth), past the clock tower (toilets here) and the St Day Inn. Turn right along Telegraph Street (notice the slate-hung houses on the corner, and other attractive cottages on the left later). A new road, also on the left, has been named after Wheal Gorland (*). Eventually you reach Scorrier Street; here go right, past a cul-de-sac, formerly Simmons' Street but now called Mills Street: see the plaque, and the earlier note about Mills' Hall.

10 Immediately beyond Mills Street, turn left on a track – not named, but known locally as Barracks Lane because the Salvation Army barracks once stood beside it. Just beyond the last house, notice the open mineshaft on the left. I was told it is at least 500 feet deep, and used to act as the main storm drain for St Day until recent changes resulting from subsidence on nearby Telegraph Hill. A little further on, look left beyond the hedge on the far side of the field, and you will see a concrete structure, one of the few surviving relics of an overhead cable system by which ore from Park-an-Chy Mine was carried down to the Poldice valley for processing (see page 10). Cross the main road with care and continue down the track almost opposite; notice the tall, graceful stack of Killifreth engine house (colour photograph 10) in the distance.

11 Beyond the attractively restored Old Coach House, turn right among the houses at Little Beside, and keep to the main track as it bears left. At the cross-tracks, where there is a house called Kernyk, turn right. You are now on the trackbed of the Poldice Tramway (see Walk 2); the open space on the right just before you reach the road was the storage yard at its terminus. At the road turn left for Wheal Unity Gate.

The "old" church at St. Day

ST DAY

Once St Day boasted thirteen pubs and its market "was a big affair with a particularly lively time on pay-days, when the miners consumed huge quantities of beef and onions accompanied by heavy draughts of ale and beer.   The celebrations often continued from Saturday afternoon to Monday evening.   The women also enjoyed themselves in a milder form holding on their pay day a monthly Kitty Bay Fair – with stalls around the account house."   (C.C.James: *A History of the Parish of Gwennap*). An excellent symbol of the change in the town's fortunes since then is the "old" church .... not so very old, because it was built in 1828.   John Betjeman described the St Day of that period as "the capital of the tin mining district" – not an exaggeration, perhaps, but as Allen Buckley has pointed out, rather than "tin" Betjeman should have said "copper".   A church big enough to seat 1,500 was essential.   Now it is a sad ruin: it was condemned as unsafe in 1956; the roof fell in in 1985, and the famous "Gothick" tower will inevitably follow suit before very long unless plans to raise £750,000 for restoration bear fruit .... but no-one I have spoken to recently in St Day seems to have much hope of that. A little booklet available in the new church opposite gives a few details about the sixth century monk who founded the original Chapel here, and mentions how it became an important shrine on the pilgrim route to St Michael's Mount.   Charles Henderson states that the shrine of the Holy Trinity survived until the reign of Queen Elizabeth I, and that the chapel at Scorrier House includes "a large crocketed pinnacle" from St Day Chapel, dating from the 15th century. Most Christmases I have a reminder of St Day's part in the history of Christianity in Cornwall when the choir I belong to sings the Sans Day Carol: "Now the holly bears a berry..." (Bernadette Fallon tells me that "Sans Day Carol" is an error in the carol books, and its true name is "St Day Carol".)   The St Day Feast is held on the third Monday after Whit each year: there are parades led by the local band, and a dance; traditionally, the youngest children receive a saffron bun, older ones a shilling (50p nowadays), and the old-age pensioners a tea-party.   The town is well worth exploring for the Georgian and Victorian houses and shop-fronts, and the granite clock tower.   Annie Trevithick's tiny history of St Day (about 1890) says that it was erected in 1831, whereas C.C.James gives 1921, and according to *The Redruth Town Trail Walkabout* (1988) the wooden structure at the top was brought here from Redruth in 1904.   The mines helped to promote other local industries, such as an important brick works (from 1860 to 1912) and a factory manufacturing fuses for detonating gunpowder (from about 1870 to shortly before 1950).   These days, instead of benefiting the town, the old mines have brought the constant threat of subsidence.   There have been several cases of holes suddenly appearing to reveal long-forgotten shafts, and one such almost led to the permanent closure of Telegraph Hill.   A local committee was formed to fight this plan, a public enquiry took place, and the road was saved .... for the time being, at least ....

WHEAL GORLAND

This was another "very ancient and rich copper mine" (C.C.James), particularly famous for the beautiful and rare mineral specimens found in it: see the note on Wheal Unity, page 6. The Wheal Gorland dumps used to be a favourite hunting-ground for collectors of minerals, but during the 1970s the dumps were removed, thus at a stroke greatly increasing the cash value of specimens already found. A recreation ground has taken the place of the dumps. Before the mine closed in 1864, its workings had reached a depth of about 1,100 feet. As with the nearby Park-an-Chy mine, parts of Gorland were re-opened early this century for the recovery of wolfram and tin: see the end of the note on Poldice Mine, page 10.

FOLLOWING THE RAILWAY TRACK THROUGH CARHARRACK

It crossed Fore Street before you reach the Mills' Hall, ran along what is now Croft Row, behind the site of the Hall and the long terrace of cottages on Fore Street, crossed the main road at Railway Terrace (its course is clearly visible on the right of the 30 m.p.h. sign, between two high walls), then passed close behind the shops. It crossed Chapel Terrace, and the next section of its track is now occupied by modern bungalows. Beyond them, a rusty old lamp standard marks its course. It crossed Wheal Damsel Road, ran in front of what was then the Steam Engine pub, crossed the road and went under the footbridge, then on below the slopes of Carn Marth to Redruth and Wheal Buller. (All that is the result of my own detective work; if your researches lead you to different conclusions, I'd be very interested to hear from you.)

Wheal Unity Wood (Walk 2) — pumping engine house on left

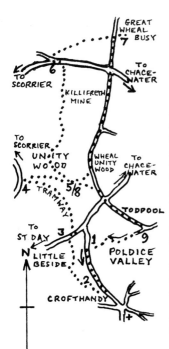

NO. 2: UNITY WOOD, KILLIFRETH, WHEAL BUSY AND TODPOOL

Nearly 5 miles,
or can be shortened to about 2½.

If you have time to do only one of the longer walks in this book, this is the one I'd recommend. It falls into three roughly equal parts: first, the best-preserved section of old tramway I have seen in Cornwall (except, perhaps, in the Luxulyan Valley: see Around the River Fowey, Walk 12); second, an attractive wood containing an amazing concentration of mineshafts; and finally, a succession of splendid engine houses and other mine buildings which it would be hard to match anywhere. It is quite an easy walk, mostly on wide tracks and quiet roads, but in wet weather you would probably need boots in a few parts of the valley below Unity Wood. The shorter route omits the woodland walk and all but two of the engine houses. There is no pub or shop along the way.

1 From Wheal Unity Gate, walk south along the road, towards Crofthandy, and take the third track on the right, marked Little Beside, which cuts back sharply and runs north-west. (Just before you turn on to it, it's worth taking a look at the big open shaft beside the road on the left.) The track follows the course of the Poldice/Portreath Tramway (*), and the open space on the left at the start is the site of the storage yard and coal pit which marked its southern terminus. One wall remains of the old weighbridge house. Bear right, past a house called "Silverlea" where home-made honey is sometimes on sale.

2 Where another track crosses, it would be possible to continue straight ahead, keeping to the tramway route, but soon that becomes very rough and runs beside an ugly car-dump, so I recommend you to turn left, and follow the main track as it bears right and passes among the cottages of Little Beside. At the T-junction turn right. Where the track meets the road, there is a long bungalow on the left. This is on the site of the Unity Fuse Works, mentioned near the end of the note on St Day (Walk 1), and in fact is probably the original main building of it.

3 At the road go right for a few yards, then take the public footpath on the left, signed Zimapan. Now you are back on the tramway, and this is an exceptionally well preserved section of it, with many obvious setts still in position. Follow the line of setts as it forks left from the main track. Ahead is the tall, graceful stack of Killifreth Mine, and to the right are the twin engine houses of Wheal Unity Wood (colour photograph 6). At the point where you are nearest to those, and also close to a new wooden farm building in the field on the right, notice how the lines of setts diverge at a passing-place. Just below the farm building is a newly-excavated area. Cross the stile just before the pond - though after the summer of 1990 it was bone dry - and continue ahead beside the wall,

THE POLDICE / PORTREATH TRAMWAY

This was the first railway to be laid above ground in Cornwall. (The first recorded use of railways underground in Cornwall was in a tin mine, Happy-Union streamwork, near Pentewan on the south coast in 1783.) Work on laying the track began at Portreath in 1809, and the complete four-mile line was in use by 1819. Until then, most of the minerals had been transported over unmade roads by trains of mules and horses with panniers. It was the great expansion of copper mining that promoted railways, because huge tonnages of copper ore had to be transported to South Wales for smelting, since Cornwall has no coal of its own, and copper smelting required much more coal than tin smelting. In addition, the mines were beginning to import larger and larger quantities of coal as the use of steam-engines increased. The Williams family, whose home was and still is Scorrier House, hidden among the woods just south of the A30, were part-owners of several mines, notably Poldice, and they had the railway built to serve these mines. Although the southern terminus of the line was at Crofthandy, where a storage yard was built, it appears that in 1819 branch lines were laid extending to United Mines and Wheal Maid (both included in Walk 4). The gauge was about four feet, and horses drew the wagons, which did not have flanged wheels but ran on rails shaped like an L in cross-section. These were attached to two lines of granite blocks, known as setts, by means of iron "chairs"; there were no sleepers between the rails, as on modern railways, because they would have impeded the horses. By 1855 the tramway had begun to fall into disrepair, partly because of the problems in using Portreath harbour, which is extremely dangerous for a ship to enter in rough weather. Long before then, most of the ore was being carried south to Devoran by the Redruth and Chasewater Railway: see the note in Walk 1. The exact date when the Portreath line closed is uncertain, but it may well have coincided with the closure of Poldice in 1873. The Portreath Tramway never transported paying passengers, but a carriage or wagon built to carry four Directors has survived and can be seen at the Geevor Mining Museum; according to John Stengelhofen in *Cornwall's Railway Heritage* (Twelveheads Press), this is "probably the oldest railway passenger vehicle in the world." For a detailed account of the history of the Portreath Tramway, see the second volume of D.B.Barton's *Essays in Cornish Mining History*. Walks covering most of the tramway north of the A30 are included in *A View from Carn Brea*.

still following the course of the tramway. The pond was dug only recently. Notice, near the start of the wall, the low arch: could this have been built for the leat carrying water from Pednandrea to Wheal Unity? (See the last part of the note on that mine, page 6.) Just beyond the arch there was obviously another passing-place on the tramway. Close to the road there's a narrow gap to squeeze through. (At present it's not possible to follow the next part of the tramway, because it passes through the private grounds of Scorrier House.)

4 Rather than continuing to the road, turn sharp right on the track running beside Unity Wood, passing the pond again. (The wood's earlier name, by the way, was Killifreth or Killefreth, meaning "the speckled grove".) Some parts along here are likely to be muddy, and in wet periods the pond sometimes floods over on to this track. Various unofficial paths and tracks go up into the wood, and about 75 yards beyond a small quarry or shaft there's a stile, but the path is overgrown here.

5 A few yards beyond that, there's a pair of granite gate-posts on the left and a clear path between them; for the full 5-mile walk, turn on to this. *(To shorten the walk, continue straight on along the narrower track running uphill to the pair of engine houses. From there, return by the same route to the main track and pick up the directions at point 8.)* The path, quite rough in places, runs up through Unity Wood, and almost everywhere you look there are capped shafts or other signs of mining activity, old workings of both Killifreth and Unity Wood mines, and before them of North Wheal Unity and Wheal Union. Fork right at both the points where there is a choice, and you should eventually reach a stile on the left of a gate. Immediately before it are ruined buildings: on the left, probably a tiny cottage, and on the right massive foundations, perhaps of stamps. After crossing the stile you can see the remains of at least six mine buildings. From left to right: Hawke's Shaft pumping engine house, an ivy-covered wall of a winding engine house (all that remained after it was used as a target for shooting practice during World War Two), the Old Sump Shaft pumping engine house and the stamps engine house, all from Killifreth Mine; further away, two stacks of arsenic works, the left-hand one at Wheal Busy and the right another part of Killifreth. Continue ahead, over another stile beside a gate, past some ruined buildings which housed a horizontal engine for winding during the last period of working, and soon you reach the restored pumping-engine house at Hawke's Shaft, Killifreth (*). Its stack, 100 feet high, is almost certainly the tallest surviving in Cornwall. Continue along the track and over the stile to the main Chacewater – Scorrier road. The ruined engine house to the left, looking like a pair of horns, is at the Black Dog Shaft of Wheal Busy. I believe it was another victim of a military exercise.

6 Go a few yards to the left and cross (please be careful: the traffic along here is often fast) to the side road opposite, but then immediately turn right past a bungalow and along the track. Cross the minor road and continue ahead to the buildings of Great Wheal Busy (*).

7 Return to the minor road and turn left (south). Soon on the left you will reach the stack and other remains of an arsenic works. These are well worth close inspection: they include a "lambreth" flue and unusually well preserved Brunton calciners dating from 1907. J.H.Trounson's *Mining in Cornwall* Vol. 2 has some interesting photographs taken here during and just after the building of the arsenic works (photographs 69-76). For some details about arsenic production, see the note on Poldice, page 9. Continue to the main road and cross it (with care again), then go on in the same direction along the road signposted to Todpool. This takes you past an arsenic calciner and stack, at the corner, and two impressive engine houses, all relics of Killifreth mine. The ivy-covered engine house on the left housed a 32" engine for the stamps (photograph on page 12), and the recently restored one on the right, at Old Sump Shaft, contained a 50" pumping engine. The fenced-off area behind the building is the site of the original boiler house; the shaft is where you would expect, beside the bob wall, but now securely capped (I hope!) and completely hidden below soil. As you continue along the road, you have a wide view embracing Unity Wood on your right, the outskirts of Chacewater to the left, and on the skyline ahead St Day Church, the Consols clock tower and a restored engine house on United Downs. After about half a mile you come to the fine pair of engine houses at Wheal Bush Farm. These are relics of Wheal

KILLIFRETH MINE
(Colour photograph 10.)

Killifreth Mine produced copper between 1826 and 1860 and tin after 1864. A lot of tin remained to be worked in 1896 when a dispute between owners and shareholders arose over plans to raise capital for new machinery; this led to closure in 1897. For a time after this it was used by the Truro Mining School. In 1911 it re-opened on an ambitious scale, when the Hawke's Shaft (sometimes called Richard's Shaft) engine house was rebuilt to take an 85" pumping engine: the brick-built upper part of the stack was doubled in height to increase the draught in the boiler fires. Arsenic was produced in the mine's latter years. Killifreth finally closed in February 1928, although there is still reported to be plenty of tin underground. In 1987–8, restoration of the Hawke's Shaft engine house was carried out as part of Carrick's Operation Engine House in conjunction with the MSC's Community Programme. In the August 1990 Newsletter of the Trevithick Society, Roger Radcliffe gives an account of the repairs carried out to the cylinder opening arch and the brick top of the stack. ("As we gazed upwards," he writes, "bracing ourselves against the stiff northerly wind, we could plainly see a block of some 30 bricks moving to and fro in sympathy with the gusts!") St Day bricks were obtained from the arsenic works at Bissoe. Mr Radcliffe points out the irony: to save one old building, another had to be robbed – but the robbing had been going on so long already at Bissoe that there was "an abundance of loose bricks". For the flying courses at the top of the stack they "not only had to be cut to a taper but chamfered into both convex and concave shapes using a template based on existing bricks." Following the successful completion of the Hawke's Shaft restoration, the same team went on to restore the engine house at Old Sump Shaft; hopes of adding the stamps engine house to the list have been set back by the cancellation of the Community Programme and by cuts resulting from the poll tax.

Killifreth Mine, from a photograph taken about 1895. L to R: Hawke's Shaft pumping engine house; winding engine house; Old Sump Shaft pumping engine house.

Unity Wood (✱): the one by the road operated both stamps and whim. Turn right down the track past the pumping engine house.

8 Take the first turning on the left, passing a house, and soon joining a minor road which brings you to a crossroads. Continue ahead into Todpool, about which there is a brief note in Walk 3.

9 Where the road bends left, turn right through Todpool Gate. The group of young trees on the bank ahead, known as the Temple Plantation from the name of a family living nearby who have been closely associated with the Poldice Valley scheme, was planted in spring 1990. Go up to the arsenic works and turn right there, then take the second track on the left, which curves right and leads to Wheal Unity Gate. If in doubt, consult the large-scale Poldice Valley map at the centre of the book. If still in doubt, you have my sympathy, and I hope it won't be me who finds your bleached bones beside some lonely spoil heap.

GREAT WHEAL BUSY

Great Wheal Busy - known in its early days as Chacewater Mine - is one of the oldest visited on walks in this book; just how old is uncertain, but we know it was active by 1718. Its importance as a copper mine was greatest during the first half of the 19th century; after that it relied more on tin and especially arsenic. The mine played a leading role in the history of the Cornish beam engine: John Smeaton erected a large Newcomen engine here in 1775, and in 1777 Busy became the first Cornish mine to install an engine designed by James Watt. In 1856 a large house was built for an 85" engine; in 1872 it was modified to take an even larger engine (90"); finally in 1909 a new 85" engine was put into it. New to Wheal Busy, that is. In fact, like so many of the great beam engines, it had been moved from place to place. This one had previously worked near Par, and then at a coal mine in South Wales. At Wheal Busy it was put to work intermittently until 1924, then lay idle for over twenty years before being broken up for scrap: see photograph No. 76 in Jack Trounson's *Mining in Cornwall* Vol. 2. The shed attached to the engine house was built to house three boilers. The nearby old building was the smithy; notice the impressive cast-iron lintels, made at Perran Foundry in 1872 when a major expansion of the workings took place. The huge burrows and surrounding land are seen by their owner, Lord Falmouth, as ripe for "development", and early in 1989 ambitious plans were published for a new town here, complete with international airport. The scheme has, to put it mildly, met with a mixed reception.

WHEAL UNITY WOOD (Drawing, page 27)

According to figures covering the period 1815 to 1903, this mine produced a large amount of copper, plus some tin and arsenic. At various times it was part of larger concerns such as St Day United and it changed its name twice: first to West Poldice and later to Tolgullow United. J.H.Collins (1912) reported, "This working is said to have given profits amounting to £60,000." The 70" pumping engine was removed to Tincroft, Camborne, when this mine closed, and worked there till about 1940. In the smaller building was a 26" engine which, according to the mining historian Ken Brown, operated stamps and also acted as a whim (winding engine), not for the shaft beside the pumping engine house but for Trefusis Shaft, quite a long distance away down in the valley.

NO. 3: CHACEWATER, TWELVEHEADS AND THE POLDICE VALLEY

Nearly 5 miles. Could be reduced to about 3½ miles if you start at Chacewater.

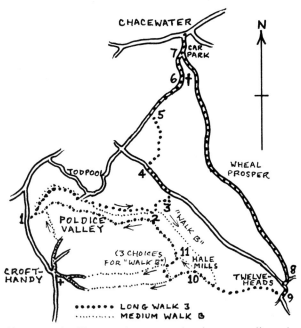

The walk to Chacewater climbs quite steeply out of the Poldice Valley by means of a path used by horses and therefore likely to be muddy; it continues along paths and wider tracks, with a little road walking. Chacewater itself is much more attractive and interesting than you would suspect if you have previously seen it only from behind car windows. From there to Twelveheads is a delightful downhill walk along a quiet road through a green and rural valley. Twelveheads, despite being overshadowed by the modern mine buildings of Mount Wellington, is a charming little hamlet, full of pretty buildings and the sounds of water. Now comes a dramatic contrast as you turn west into the valley leading to Hale Mills, the scene of so much industrial activity for many centuries, and yet it still has its pockets of greenery in which wild creatures flourish. Beyond Hale Mills, the walk route re-enters the Poldice Valley, running for some distance beside the course of a mineral tramway – part of the Redruth and Chasewater Railway's branch line which was intended to extend as far as Wheal Busy. Thus this is a very varied walk, and one which is full of interest for anyone wishing to understand the history of this important mining district. Chacewater offers a good selection of shops and pubs, plus public toilets. The public car park in Chacewater is near the start of the valley road to Twelveheads, and would make a good alternative place to begin the walk: in that case, pick up the directions at point 7. This would enable you to shorten the walk by omitting Poldice, turning up the path as described in point 2.

1 From Wheal Unity Gate take the track ahead leading towards the ruined chimney, but after a few yards turn left on a narrower track or path running beside a wire fence. Cross the track leading left to Poldice Gate, and continue beside the fence. Soon the path curves left towards the twin engine houses of Unity Wood mine and ends at a farm gate. It's worth going a few yards to the right here to look into the mouth of Todpool Shaft (page 7), now completely shrouded in lush vegetation, including willowherb, tansy, brambles, gorse, heather, various shrubs, and a sycamore growing right over the gaping hole. You now have to retrace your steps,

and when you reach the track follow it as it curves left near the arsenic works and across the floor of the valley towards the houses of Todpool (*). As you approach Todpool Gate, take the track on the right, running east along the north side of the valley. The large tips, looking almost like china clay, on the other side of the valley, are waste material from the processing of ore from Park-an-Chy mine during the late 1920s: see the note on Poldice, page 10. After about a quarter of a mile, you could take the narrow, grassy path on the left, which starts beside a small granite gate post. This soon leads back to the track at what was once Bissa Pool (page 13). The stone with the number 50 (I think) carved on it is one of many marking parish boundaries (Gwennap to the south, Chacewater - originally Kenwyn, until 1837 - to the north).

TODPOOL

Oliver Padel does not offer an explanation of this name, but the syllable "tod" elsewhere refers to "lea-land", land usually down to pasture but occasionally ploughed. Add a pool to that, and you have a very rural scene - in fact, most likely a field rather than a settlement. Presumably the hamlet was created entirely by the mines: Creegbrawse was on its doorstep, as well as Poldice and Wheal Unity. As mentioned in Walk 2, there was once a pub; there was a Methodist Chapel too, and more miners' cottages than we now see.

---

2 Just beyond that, take the path up on the left - probably muddy, I'm afraid. Soon you pass a well which looks as if it might still be in use. The path climbs quite steeply and eventually joins a stony track. Here it's worth pausing, not only to get your breath back but to admire the wide view over the Poldice Valley. In the distance, from right to left, can be seen the engine house of Grambler / St Aubyn United mine, near Gwennap Pit; St Day clock tower and church; Carn Marth; the Consols clock tower; and a restored engine house of United Mines.

3 Turn left on the track, and left again at the road. Here the view extends further east to the Wheal Fortune engine house and Mount Wellington mine.

4 After just over 200 yards, turn right on to a grassy path between hedges. From this you can see Wheal Jane to the right. Later the path joins a wider track, where you bear right, and then keep to the main track ahead.

5 Turn right on the road, which runs down into Chacewater. On the right before the church is the imposing Chacewater House, formerly the vicarage but now privately owned; the new vicarage is a modest bungalow a little way down the hill. Chacewater Church (*) is worth a visit.

6 Go on down past the school, founded by the National Schools movement in 1847. To continue the main walk route, turn right on the minor road signposted to Twelveheads; but if you're ready for refreshments or want to explore the village, go down to the main street first. (There are toilets in the car park on the right before you reach it.) Most of the terraced houses are at least 150 years old (dating, as you would expect, from the period when Cornish mining was at its most prosperous) but still in good order; only the rather hectic through-traffic tends to spoil the impression, and you can soon get away from that by taking one of the side-roads or

Directions continue on page 38.

CHACEWATER AND ITS CHURCH

Oliver Padel states that "chace" means a hunting ground, and this district belonged to Goodern Manor, otherwise known as Blanchland (see Walk 8 in *A View from Carn Marth*), which seems to have been a palace of Dark Age lords or "kings" of Cornwall. Thus Chacewater figures in the legend of Tristan and Isolda (usually called Tristram and Iseult in Cornwall) as King Mark's hunting ground, and also in the stories of cruel King Teudar who killed many Celtic saints. (Charles Henderson, writing in 1925, makes a less colourful comment: "In the Middle Ages the whole district was barren heath land, over which various Lords of Manors had 'Free Warren.'") Although farming and trades such as thatching and brewing were important to Chacewater, the village was largely created by the mines that surround it, and its fortunes have risen and fallen with theirs. Admittedly it looks quite prosperous now, despite the parlous state of Cornish mining: its pleasant setting has attracted retirement homes, and it is conveniently placed for commuting to Truro and Redruth. From about 1760, Chacewater was the home of the celebrated Hornblower family who designed and built so many of the great steam engines. (Jonathan Hornblower, 1717-80, had 13 children: Jabez, Jethro, Joanna, Jesse, Jemima, Jonathan, Joseph, Jemima [did the first Jemima die young?], Julia, Jecholia, Jedida, Jerusha and Josiah. The search for girls' names obviously grew desperate.) An entertaining and perceptive account of Chacewater by George Henwood was published in the *Mining Journal* during the late 1850s. "When the mines were in their palmy days, Chacewater was a place of considerable importance as a mining village; a capital market-house was built for the convenience of the people, but has since been almost deserted ..... Scarcely a family is to be found one member at least of whom has not been out either to Mexico, California, Brazil, New Zealand, Australia, Africa, Spain, or some mining district of less account." Great Wheal Busy had recently been re-opened, and prosperity was returning; but since the entire village belonged to Lord Falmouth and all leases were restricted to three lives, few people were prepared to build "a superior class of houses." Even so, Betjeman rightly points to its "well-built colour-washed cottages .... bow-windowed Georgian shops .... and up the valley slopes the tidy villas built in the last century by tin mine captains." Chacewater parish was carved out of Kenwyn and Kea in 1837 - evidence of the increased population brought by the mines. St Paul's Church, consecrated in the following year, was built for a congregation of 1,500. A leaflet published for the church's 150th anniversary says, "A local paper referred to it as one of the very ugliest churches in Cornwall and a previous Vicar said that he thought it was a factory when he first saw it. In 1866 the *West Briton* of the day reported: 'During the thunderstorm on Saturday last (Feb. 3rd) Chacewater Church which has recently been repaired, was struck by lightning which split the wall from ground to roof. Several windows were smashed into hundreds of pieces, being hurled from the west end up to the pulpit, a distance of 90 feet.' Of this original Church only the lofty tower with battlements, the second highest in Cornwall, now remains. The Church was rebuilt and completed in 1892 from the design of Edward Sedding of Plymouth. There was no gallery and the seating capacity was reduced to 500." That last sentence is again symptomatic of the fortunes of the mines. Incidentally, the highest church tower in Cornwall is that of Grampound, and the claim to the second highest is also made by St Columb Minor.

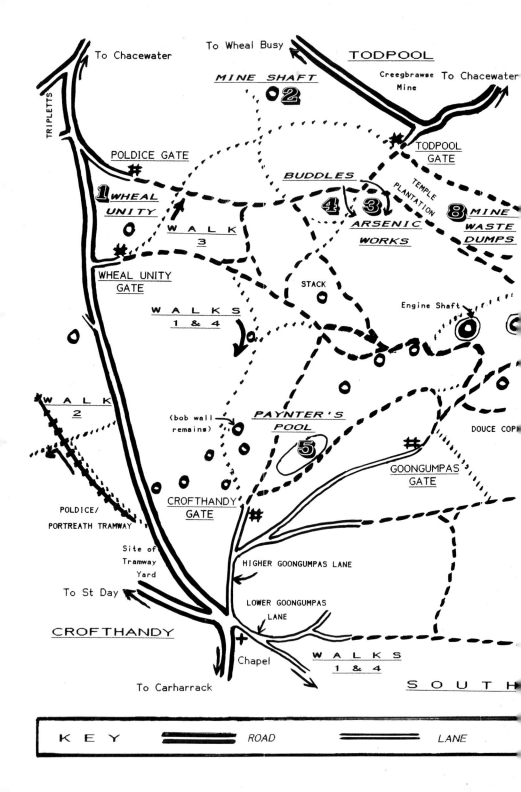

The Poldice Valley

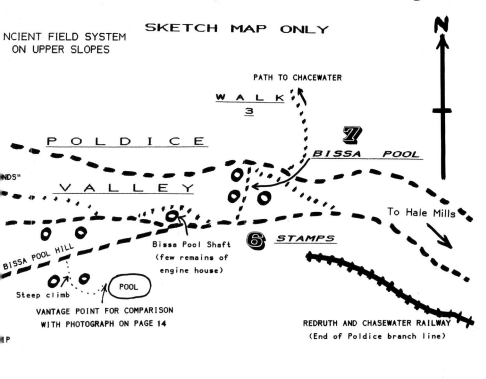

NCIENT FIELD SYSTEM
ON UPPER SLOPES

N

PATH TO CHACEWATER

W A L K
3

P O L D I C E

7

BISSA   POOL

NDS"

V A L L E Y

To Hale Mills

BISSA POOL HILL

Bissa Pool Shaft
(few remains of
engine house)

6   *STAMPS*

POOL

Steep climb

VANTAGE POINT FOR COMPARISON
WITH PHOTOGRAPH ON PAGE 14

REDRUTH AND CHASEWATER RAILWAY
(End of Poldice branch line)

P

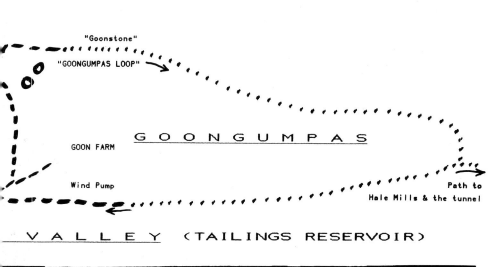

"Goonstone"

"GOONGUMPAS LOOP"

G O O N G U M P A S

GOON FARM

Wind Pump

Path to
Hale Mills & the tunnel

V A L L E Y   (TAILINGS RESERVOIR)

▬ ▬ ▬ ▬ *TRACK*	,,,,,,,, *PATH*	⬤ *MINE SHAFT*

paths on the far side of the main street. Chacewater Post Office was run by Mrs Annette Penhaligon until her husband David was re-elected as MP for Truro in 1979. There are three pubs, all said to be friendly. David Guthrie describes The Rambling Miner as "Very, very old-fashioned – proper Cornish." The King's Head is the only one I can report on from personal experience. The main room is decorated with mining photographs and collections of minerals, many of them from Wheal Jane, and the dining area is fitted out as a scene "down the mine". "'Ave you 'Ad it in our Adit?" reads the sign above the entrance. "Sample mine host's Daily Dish." We didn't venture into the dark recesses of the Adit, but enjoyed a tasty and reasonably-priced meal in a pleasant atmosphere.

7 The valley road sloping gently down to Twelveheads is pretty and usually very little used by motor vehicles. I last walked it quite early on a Sunday morning in April, and the list in my notebook revives for me the pleasures of the experience: "Glossy leaves on trees....Glimpse of church....Blackthorn, chickens, pigs, ducks, cows, friendly dogs, a dung-spreader, stream, ponds (for fish-breeding?)...." A sign announces the Chacewater Vineyard, but where are the vines? The same sign refers to a herb and garden nursery, geese and cider. Just to the right is an older notice, "Tippett's Stamps Nurseries" – a timely reminder that when the mines were in full swing this was a very different place, because the clatter of Cornish Stamps in operation must have been almost unbearable. The stamps probably processed ore from Creegbrawse mine, just above Todpool, if I am right in guessing that Tippett was an official there: two shafts at Creegbrawse are named after him. Nearby, just a little way up the slope on the other side of the stream, was a small copper mine, one of many in Cornwall given the optimistic name of Wheal Prosper. Evidently it failed to live up to expectations: its recorded output is unimpressive. It closed in 1870, and it is hard now to find any surface remains. The stream presumably provided the power to drive Tippett's Stamps, and still today it is being harnessed to drive a small waterwheel. Shortly after you have passed the track going up on the right to Rising Sun farm (perhaps once a beer-house, judging by its name), you could make a very short diversion by crossing the bridge on the left; notice the small leat which has been taken off the stream beside the bridge. Walk along the track or road on the far side of the stream for a few yards, then turn right on a footpath just beyond a corrugated building; this takes you back over the stream and past the lightweight, undershot waterwheel, apparently being used to generate electricity. Turn left at the road to continue down the valley towards Twelveheads (*).

TWELVEHEADS

Few if any Cornish place-names give so clear an indication as this of a community's having been created by the mining industry – although of course there may have been an earlier name before the days of twelve-headed Cornish Stamps machines. It is an ideal spot for a settlement: a sheltered, fertile valley where two streams meet, providing ample power for mills as well as stamps.

8 At the T-junction turn right into the village, then first left, signposted Point Mills, Bissoe. Soon you pass the Methodist Church. Look right to see Twelveheads Mill, now almost completely rebuilt after a long period of neglect.

9 After crossing the bridge over the Carnon River, at the point where the road bends left, turn right along a wide track, passing the sign announcing that this is the Twelveheads Gate of the Poldice Valley. You now have a clearer view of the mill building. This part of the Bissoe Valley makes an interesting contrast with the valley running down from Chacewater. At this point it is still mainly green, but already the signs of industry are evident, especially up to the left and along the valley-bottom, where there is a line of mine shafts. More and more as you walk on, the patches of green give way to the dereliction which is a legacy of the days when this valley could lay claim to the title of Copper Capital of the World; it takes a strong effort of imagination to picture it as it must have been before its mineral wealth was exploited. Notice the rusty-yellowish deposits of ochre (*) on the banks of the stream. As you

---

OCHRE

This mustard-coloured or reddish substance, a blend of iron oxide and fine clay, seems to be a major ingredient of the tailings from Mount Wellington and the water issuing from the County Adit. Several small enterprises were set up in the Carnon valley to extract the ochre for use as a pigment in paint. An Ochre Works is shown on the 1908 O.S. map, just upstream of Conn's chemical works at Bissoe.

The tunnels under the railway embankment at Hale Mills

approach the cottages at Hale Mills (see the comments in Medium-length Walk B), notice the ivy-covered chimney up on the right. This is a relic of Wheal Henry, a tin-and-copper mine of which few reliable records seem to have survived. Despite the name of its main shaft, "Goodluck", it seems never to have been very successful. Its workings included those of several small old mines, two of which were Great and Little Goodluck, and another was Killicor; the ruined engine house with its ivy-covered stack is said to have belonged to Killicor, and to be one of the oldest remnants of an engine house in the valley. Unlike most later ones, it is built of slaty stone rather than granite. See page 65. A public footpath runs up the hill beside it, but it is badly overgrown and hard to find.

10 At Hale Mills, fork left past a former miner's cottage to pass through the surprisingly long, masonry-lined tunnel through the embankment built by the Redruth and Chasewater Railway (see the note in Walk 1) to carry its branch line to Poldice Mine. The stream, now even more deeply coloured by ochre (colour photograph 5), has its own smaller tunnel. When you emerge on the far side you will see the concrete pipe by which the stream was diverted underneath the bed of the Mount Wellington tailings dam, as described in Walk 1. Take the track up on the right, and then the steep, narrow path which goes more sharply to the right, passing a walled, capped mineshaft on your left. From here you have a clear view of the railway embankment across the valley. Now the path goes right again, downhill. Soon you will come to a cutting on the left, which was excavated to take the branch line. There is no right of way along the railway trackbed – unfortunately, from a walker's point of view, but keeping people out of it protects the birds and other wildlife living in this sheltered spot, which is a green haven amidst the industrial desolation, and seems to have its own microclimate. (Colour photograph 8.) Continue down the path.

11 Turn left at the bottom, walking either along the valley bottom or on the parallel track a little higher up the slope on the left. After about half a mile you will come to an impressive wall on the left side of the upper track; above this are the massive foundations built for Cornish stamps machines, and at that point the railway trackbed seems to come to an end. Whether in fact it was ever completed as far as Poldice Mine, or even whether rails were ever laid on the branch line across the embankment at Hale Mills, are questions on which students of the railway disagree. (Barton says "the expensive earthworks languished unused" [page 54], but on the map dated 1856 [pages 42-3] it is indicated that "locomotives at present work" as far as Poldice; the rest of the "Wheal Bissy Branch" is shown as "not completed". For more about this, see page 70.) On the right nearby are more ruined mine-buildings, perhaps the remains of a stack and engine-house, together with concrete "plats" or foundations for ˙stamps, complete with a wheel-pit. From here the track goes gently uphill. Fork right and right again to pass among the castle-like ruins of the arsenic works and dressing floors of Poldice. (See the note and plan on pages 8-10.) From here, return to Wheal Unity; the map on the centre pages will, I hope, guide you through the maze of tracks.

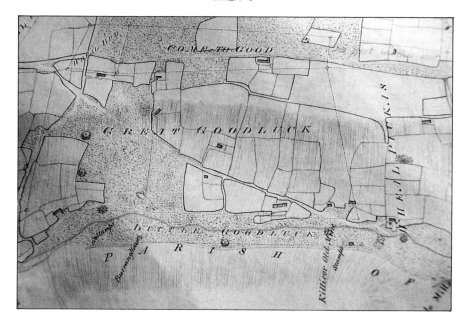

Richard Thomas is perhaps best known for his report on and map of the mining region between Camborne and Chacewater, published in 1819 (see pages 6 and 23). He was born in Falmouth but later lived in a house his father had built near the old Perran tin-smelting works in the Carnon Valley. This ceased working in 1802, but in 1812 it re-opened as the first commercial arsenic works in Britain. During the 1840s it was greatly expanded, and the noxious fumes from it made life intolerable for Thomas, who was forced to move and became a chief witness in a court case against the owner in 1851. (See D.B.Barton's *Essays in Cornish Mining History*, Volume 2.) Thomas was a civil engineer and surveyor, concerned especially with railways and mining, and the above photograph shows part of a map by him dated October 1837. So far as I know, the map is unpublished; it is owned by Mr Justin Brooke, and reproduced here with his kind permission. It shows the east end of the Poldice Valley, north of Hale (spelt "Hayle" here) Mills, and gives the names of some of the smaller mines later included in Wheal Henry: Great and Little Goodluck, Come-to-Good, Wheal Pickas and Wheal Bud. "Killicor Old Mine", together with two sets of stamps and a burning house (see page 9), are indicated in the valley marking the boundary of the Parish of Gwennap at the bottom of the photograph. Running diagonally from bottom-right to top-left is a track still marked on the OS maps as a public footpath, but now overgrown near the bottom; the path used in point 2 of this walk joins it near the top, and the road referred to in point 3 is shown very faintly on the map (probably too faintly to appear on this copy), running parallel with the top of the photograph through Wheal Bud and Come-to-Good.

NO. 4: THE SOUTH VALLEY, BISSOE, FROGPOOL AND WHEAL FORTUNE OR UNITED DOWNS

Nearly 7 miles.

This walk is full of interest and variety, since it includes a valley intensively exploited by industry over many centuries, an important section of the track of one of the early mineral railways, four former watermills with their leats, beautiful countryside which feels a world away from mines and railways, and finally a look at the surface remains of two of the world's greatest copper mines, United and Consols. Although quite a long walk, it is mostly easy going (the only slight exception to that is the path between Coombe and Frogpool, which is hilly and includes some awkward stiles and various minor obstacles), and there is a good pub conveniently placed at Frogpool, as well as shops at Bissoe and Frogpool. A choice of two routes is given for the later part of the walk.

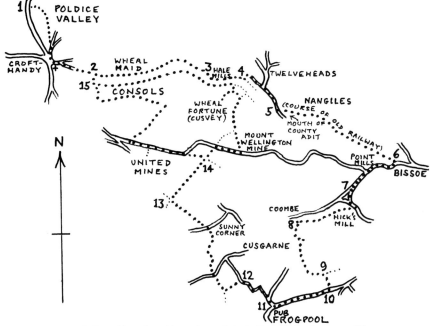

1 At the start, follow the directions in point 1 for Walk 1, page 21.

2 At the stile go straight ahead, down to the valley-floor – in fact, the area excavated as the tailings reservoir for Mount Wellington Mine (*), crossed by three dam walls. Continue on the left (north) side of the valley, sometimes at the higher level. This area is part of the sett of Wheal Maid (*). As you approach the last dam wall, notice the pool in the valley bottom, stained amazing shades of gold, mustard and red by the ochre and other minerals that settled out into the ground here when Mount Wellington was active. (In dry weather there may be no pool, but the colours remain.) Beyond the last dam wall, the stream which was taken underneath the tailings reservoir by means of a concrete conduit emerges briefly to the light before flowing through the short tunnel under the old Redruth and Chasewater Railway embankment (see Walk 3).

MOUNT WELLINGTON MINE

An old mine called Wheal Friendship, part of United Mines, was previously on this site. It was last worked by two brothers called Wellington during the 1930s, and the modern mine is named after them; locally, though, it is sometimes known as Magpie Mine. Following the rise in world tin prices during the 1960s, several new mining ventures were launched in Cornwall; Wheal Jane, between Twelveheads and Baldhu, was the first, in 1971, and Mount Wellington began full production in 1976. By that year the main shaft was already about a thousand feet deep, and the aim was to treat 600 tonnes of ore per day, using a work-force of about 300. Prices collapsed in 1985, and Mount Wellington closed. Jane continued to function on a reduced scale, and since its workings are linked with Wellington's, the latter also remained viable in case of a revival in the industry's fortunes. Early in 1989, tin prices rose, but this was a false dawn, and at the time of writing (October 1990) the final closure of Wheal Jane within the next few months seems inevitable.

WHEAL MAID

This old copper mine, sometimes called Wheal Maiden, was at various periods linked with East Wheal Damsel and Carharrack Mine, both a little further east, and in 1864 it was combined with Poldice, Unity and Gorland to form St Day United Mines. All this makes it difficult to say how successful it was, but J.H.Collins notes that "The profits from 1800 to 1840 are said to have reached £200,000." It figures in the history books as the first Cornish mine to erect a "steam whim", a beam engine adapted for rotary use (1784).

3 Cross to the far (south) side of the valley, either along the top of the dam wall or by going down to the stream and up the bank beyond, and turn left along the main trackbed of the Redruth and Chasewater Railway. It is easily recognised by the black pipe that runs along it (this brought the tailings from the mine to the reservoir); and if you look carefully you will see several granite setts, confirming that this was indeed the railway. Some of the setts are half-buried, but large numbers have been dug up and are scattered around or piled in heaps. The bridge carrying a farm track over the line seems to have been constructed partly of old rails, but I believe the bridge deck was rebuilt in the 1930s, so they are unlikely to be from the mineral railway. Eventually a second line of black pipes appears beside the first.

4 Take the track on the left soon after that, which brings you down to the unsurfaced road running along the valley bottom, and turn right on that. You are now entering Twelveheads village (see the note in Walk 3), and soon on the left is a former watermill which was being restored – in fact, almost totally rebuilt – early in 1990. At the surfaced road, continue ahead, with the buildings of Mount Wellington mine looming above on the right. Walk on till you pass the last house (on the right, under a power cable).

5 Turn left just beyond that, and now you are following the course of the mineral railway again, on the embankment by which it crossed the Carnon Valley. Before walking over that you could go down beside the Carnon

stream to see where the County Adit (*) comes to surface; on the left nearby is the fine bridge under the embankment (colour photograph 7). Then continue along the embankment, with a view up the side-valley left to Twelveheads. Keep left at the first junction and right at the second to stay on the railway trackbed. You should see a considerable number of setts: in one place there is a line of at least nine on the right-hand side, and just beyond them you can see where there was a loop on the left. High up on the left are the dumps and the last remnants of the once-impressive engine house of Nangiles mine (*). Towards the far end of the valley, as you approach Bissoe (*), some attempts have been made at landscaping and replanting, but this scheme will presumably soon be overtaken by the more dramatic one, permission for which has been granted despite determined opposition by local residents. This is for the drilling

---

THE COUNTY ADIT

Most mineral veins or "lodes" in Cornwall run at a steep angle from the surface, some almost vertically, so the longer a mine is active the deeper its workings and the greater the problem of pumping water out of them. By 1730, Poldice Mine was already becoming too deep for the engines available, and in 1748 (rather than 1784, as stated by Peter Stanier) its manager, John Williams, along with its chief "adventurer" or shareholder, William Lemon, started the construction of a deep drainage outlet or "adit" coming to surface in the valley below Nangiles Mine near Twelveheads. By 1768 the adit reached the western side of the Poldice sett; ten years later a branch ran through Great Wheal Busy to Wheal Peevor (now easily recognisable by the impressive group of three engine houses beside the A30). Eventually the County or Great Adit, with its many side branches, was nearly forty miles in length, drained over thirty square miles and served about fifty mines. (C.C.James lists many, if not all, of them, and explains how they were linked: page 177.) The kind of benefit it brought is indicated by this extract from a letter written about 1793 about a planned extension: "You will get under two capital old tin mines, viz. Wheal Radnor and Wheal Prussia, and will assuredly have much tin from each. As the expense of drawing the water the last time they were wrought was very great - and yet much money got, they will be likely to turn in profit when the adit is brought to them which will be deeper than any part of their present workings." (Quoted by A.K.H.Jenkin) Having many mines draining into one adit could also bring serious problems: Cyril Noall tells how in 1872 a blockage in the County Adit at the abandoned Wheal Damsel threatened to cause flooding at Poldice, and four men who were investigating the problem very narrowly escaped with their lives when the blockage gave way releasing some 3,000 cubic fathoms of water which poured down one shaft "with a roar like that of the Falls of Niagara." (*Cornish Mine Disasters*, Truran 1989. The same story was told by John Vivian in *Tales of the Cornish Miners*, Tor Mark, 1970.) The average depth of the adit is about 160 feet, but it is at least 400 feet down in some places, such as at Wheal Hope (West Wheal Damsel). Additions and improvements to the system, such as the driving of a second adit to cope with the increased water flow as more mines were added and the original ones were extended, continued till about 1870, and even during the last few years work has been carried out to clear rock falls near the original portal below Mount Wellington and construct new outlets.

Twelveheads as seen from the Redruth & Chasewater Railway

of what is claimed will be the deepest hole ever bored in Britain, over 4½ miles, in pursuit of "hot rocks". Research along similar lines has been carried out for several years near Stithians. Just how much of the site of the old hardcore plant, formerly Conn's Chemical Works, and the waste ground beside the road and on the north side of the stream will be occupied by these works I don't know, but I understand that the railway trackbed will be untouched, so you should encounter no difficulties in continuing straight along that to the road, which you reach opposite the entrance to Cornish Concrete Products.

6 A short way along the road to the left is the post office and general stores, where you could buy provisions (and Landfall Walks Books!); but to go on with the walk, turn right. The road is quite busy, so do please use the verge wherever possible. This was once an area rich in watermills, and on the right just past the bridge is one of them, Point Mills. The tall, tapering stack on the left is a relic of the most important of several arsenic works which operated at Bissoe until well into this century. (For some comments on arsenic production in Cornwall, see the note on Poldice Mine, pages 8-10.) The land south and east of the stack and ruined lambreth flues is on lease to the Cornwall Trust for Nature Conservation, who are making valiant efforts to replant, despite a concentration of arsenic in the soil said to be the highest anywhere in the world. The most barren areas are being capped with a layer of mud dredged from the Fal estuary. You are free to walk up to the ruined buildings if you wish, but beware of approaching too close to the stack, which is becoming more and more rickety. Continue along the road, past Richards' filling station.

NANGILES MINE

"A very ancient mine" (Collins), Nangiles recorded production of over 3,000 tons of copper, plus smaller amounts of tin, iron, zinc, arsenic and ochre, between 1845 and 1906. (These figures are complicated by the fact that Nangiles worked with Wheal Andrew, on the opposite side of the valley, and later became part of a larger group called Falmouth Consolidated Mines.) The water in this mine is said to have contained so much vitriol (sulphuric acid) that it would "rot a pair of boots off a man's feet in one day". As a result it was necessary to line the pumps with wood and brass or bronze, and the cost of this ruined the company. (D.B.Barton mentions another remedy for acid water in boilers: "the addition of a quantity of potatoes at monthly intervals.") A unique feature at Nangiles is a railway with wooden lines seventy feet underground, and again it is thought that wood was chosen because of the acid; this seems to be confirmed by the discovery of a boot with wooden "nails" in one of the workings. (*Journal of the Trevithick Society,* 1977) The fine engine-house on the ridge top was largely destroyed in the 1960s, and now there remains only the bob wall, the thick wall which supported the beam of the pumping engine. Nangiles was last re-worked as recently as 1967.

BISSOE

The name means "birch trees", and hints at a rural past which seems unlikely ever to return, despite all efforts by planters and other conservationists. Even less likely is its revival as a port. There is a strong tradition that in medieval times tin was shipped from Bissoe, but tin streaming in the Carnon Valley greatly accelerated the natural silting-up process and cut the village off from tidal waters - a fate similar to those of Tregony, Ruan Lanihorne and Treesmill, and to a lesser extent Devoran, Truro and Lostwithiel.

7 Turn left at the sign, Hick's Mill, Coldwind Cross. As you do so, notice the well-preserved leat beside the road. Turn right immediately beyond Hick's Mill, now named The Old Mill. One of its two waterwheels, in quite a good state of preservation, is on this (south) side of the mill, but the fir trees may hide it now; the other, of which little remains, is at right angles to it, on the west side. The leat is in good order, and the system of launders leading the water to the wheels is still more-or-less intact. The path passes Hick's Mill Church and then runs beside the leat and the stream, soon crossing the leat. Immediately beyond the weir in the stream it crosses back.

8 Just past that point, turn left on a track or lane which goes quite steeply uphill. After the first gate at "The Hay Barn", turn right through a small gate (there is a footpath sign on the wall), then left among outbuildings. You pass through another small metal gate and a wooden farm gate ahead, then turn right and go through another wooden farm gate. Now, unless you got lost somewhere among all those gates, you should be walking with a hedge on your right. Go through the gap on the left of the low wall ahead (when we were there, the gap was partly blocked by an old bedstead, and there was a single strand of barbed wire on the far side), and continue on the left side of the hedge as before. The view to the

right now is of Cusgarne in the valley below, and in the distance Carn Marth, with Pennance Mine engine house on the slope; the hill to the left of that, with a mast on it, is Carnkie (pronounced to rhyme with "eye"). Continue past a farm building, cross the stile on the right, and then go left, uphill, along the lane.

9 After the left bend, don't miss the stile on the right, just before the remains of a gate with two granite gate-posts. (If you pass some beehives and a small building on the left, you've missed the stile.... We did!) The path now crosses the field to another stile with a rusty gate in front of it, and continues in the same line to a third stile at the road. Take care at this one: don't jump in front of a car.

10 Turn right into Frogpool. If you're ready for refreshments, I can thoroughly recommend the food and the friendly atmosphere at the Cornish Arms; alternatively, there's a well-stocked and equally friendly general store next door.

11 Turn right at the pub, then first left on to a very minor and twisty road. Continue on this for about a quarter of a mile.

12 Turn left on a wide track running between hedges, and at the T-junction go right. This leads down to another minor road and another mill: a millstone and part of the leat can be seen on the left. Continue ahead over the

Hick's Mill

stream by ford or footbridge, and up the stony track past the attractive old building of Cusgarne Manor Farm. Bear right, climbing quite steeply up to join the road at Rose Cottage. This is known as Sunny Corner. There turn left and immediately right on to a track.

13 At the crosstracks beside a cottage, turn right, and at the road continue in the same direction.

14 When you reach another crosstracks, you have a choice of routes:

BACK TO THE SOUTH VALLEY This is the more attractive route scenically, giving fine views across the valley and the chance of a close look at Wheal Fortune engine house. For this, read on after the next paragraph.

ACROSS UNITED DOWNS This route keeps to the high, open land and includes some road walking. Several ruined engine houses of United Mines are passed, and one which has been restored can be visited. If this is your choice, turn left, and at the road continue ahead. You are now on United Downs, and the well-restored engine house on the left, which is worth close inspection, was one of several built by United Mines (*). This particular building was erected at the start of this century, when attempts were made to extract tin from the burrows (dumps) and shallower underground workings of the old mines. It housed a 34-inch engine which operated ore-crushing machinery consisting of 120 stampheads. A short way past the turning to the engine house, a copse on the left hides from view the buildings of Tregarlands Farm. In the days when Consols and United flourished this was a pub, The Miners' Arms; it is still given that name on the 1908 O.S. map. Take the track sharp right shortly before Tregarlands. Now on the left you have a good view of Carharrack and St Day. Continue past the line of explosives containers and take the next turning left (with a fence on the left, and newly planted – in 1990 – conifers also on that side), which soon brings you to the remains of the clock tower of Great Consolidated Mines (Consols) (*). (Little seems to be known about the history of the clock tower *(drawing: page 71)*. Mr Eric Rabjohns tells me that Lt. Cmdr. Joe Mills of St Day has in his possession the clock mechanism. Lt. Cmdr. Mills believes that the same mechanism was once housed in the St Day clock tower. He thinks it was not in John Taylor's nature to erect anything so frivolous as a clock tower, and that the Consols building therefore probably dates from before 1819. By the same token, of course, it could be post-1839, and to me that seems more likely: the building does not look particularly ancient, and it does not seem to be shown on the engraving on page 57, which must be no earlier than 1828, when St Day church was built.) From there, go right, towards the old stack and ruined engine house. These, described by Peter Stanier as "among the oldest in Cornwall", are relics of Wheal Virgin. Just before them, go left, then curve right, down to the dam embankment at the western end of the tailings reservoir. Return to the starting point as described in point 15.

FOR THE VALLEY ROUTE, go straight on at the crosstracks, down an attractive path between hedges. At the road, you could continue straight ahead down the track signed Cusvey Bungalow, and take the footpath straight ahead at the point where the track curves left and right, but when I walked this in September it was quite badly overgrown. Turn left on the track at the bottom. For an easier route, turn right at the road,

CONSOLS AND UNITED MINES

The small area south of Goongumpas, and stretching roughly from Carharrack in the west to Mount Wellington Mine in the east, has been intensively mined for a very long time, and during the second half of the 18th century at least a dozen mines here proved very rich in copper. By about 1780 one group (Virgin, West Virgin, Girl, Maid and Fortune with Cusvey; Barton also mentions Carharrack Mine) had amalgamated as Great Consolidated Mines, and another including Poldory, Ale and Cakes and Wheal Cupboard had become United Mines. In 1787 the novelist William Beckford visited Consols and wrote this description: "At every step one stumbles upon ladders that lead into utter darkness or funnels that exhale warm copperous vapours. All around these openings the ore is piled up in heaps ready for purchasers. I saw it drawn reeking out of the mine by the help of a machine called a whim put in motion by mules, which in their turn are stimulated by impish children hanging over the poor brutes and flogging them without respite. The dismal scene of whims, suffering mules and hillocks of cinders, extends for miles. Huge iron engines creaking and groaning invented by Watt and tall chimneys smoking and flaming, that seem to belong to Old Nicholas's abode, diversify the prospect." Beckford contrasts the mine officials who "regale upon beef, pudding and brandy" with the miners, "woeful figures in tattered garments with pickaxes on their shoulders," who "crawled out of a dark fissure and repaired to a hovel, which I learnt was a gin-shop." Towards the end of the century, competition mainly from Anglesey caused problems, and even though output was still quite high, both groups were closed in about 1805. In 1811, when Consols was described as "totally abandoned", United was re-started, and within a year or two Michael and John Williams of Scorrier were manager and purser. Soon after that, John Williams tried to form a company to re-open Consols; but in the event it was the Norwich-born John Taylor, armed with £65,000 supplied by his London shareholders, who succeeded in getting them working again, in 1819. The gamble paid off handsomely, and from 1823 to 1840 Consols' annual output of copper outstripped all its rivals, including Dolcoath. In 1824 Taylor took over United, and by 1830 the employees numbered over 3,000. In 1839 Taylor's application to renew the lease of Consols was refused, and his response was what was called "picking the eyes out of a bal", that is, he stripped the mine of all available ore including underground stockpiles. "In 1839, writes Barton, "no less than 23,194 tons of ore were sold – the greatest annual output by far ever to be recorded for any mine in Cornwall." In the following year, the figure dropped to 13,951 tons; from then on it fell steadily, and in 1843 was overtaken by United's. In 1857 United annexed Consols, and the new group, including Wheal Clifford, named itself Clifford Amalgamated. Its output during the '60s was still huge, but the great days of Cornish copper mining were over. When Clifford Amalgamated closed in 1870 it had, says Barton, "the greatest number of engines used on any Cornish mine, or indeed on any single set of mines in the world." There were over eighty miles of underground workings and eighteen engine-houses; nearly a million tons of copper, plus some tin and other metals, were brought up. Little now remains on the surface. The great waste-heaps, one of which according to Barton was "as high as Truro Cathedral", have been depleted, much of the material having been removed for road-making; some parts have been landscaped and replanted, others used as sites for modern industries.

towards Mount Wellington mine. You may notice vapours rising from a shaft quite close to the road on the left, unless by the time you come here the mine has been finally and completely shut down. Take the second track on the left, signed Old Cusvey House; this track is opposite one on the right signed White Cott, Wheal Clifford. After about a quarter of a mile you will pass a tiny old cottage and a house named Wheal Fortune. Ignore the track going right soon after this, and turn up the track on the left a few yards later, which when I walked it had recently been cleared of vegetation. It curves left, finally reaching the ivy-clad engine-house and stack of Wheal Fortune or Cusvey Mine (*). Return by the same track at first (notice what looks like an old flue on the right), but take the sharp-left turning which brings you down to the main track running westwards above the valley. From here you have a good view over the former trackbed of the mineral railway and Hale Mills, with St Day and the twin engine houses of Unity Wood mine in the distance. Soon you are overlooking the tailings dam. The track is fairly level at first, but then goes uphill. Near the top of the slope, fork right, and continue with the fence on your right, heading towards two ruined stacks and other old mine buildings, including the stump of the Consols clock tower (see previous paragraph). Where two rows of iron posts have been set up across the track, you can turn up on your left to make a closer inspection of the buildings, returning by the same route.

15 Cross the valley either along the top of the embankment or by using the path below it on the left. Go over the stile on the left and return to the car park, as at the start of the walk.

WHEAL FORTUNE (Drawing: page 1)

This was one of the old mines which became part of Consols. A story told by Cyril Noall in *Cornish Mine Disasters* gives a vivid impression of miners' working conditions. In June 1853 two miners were walking along the 120 fathom level (720 feet) when falling water put out both their candles. One set off for the 90 fathom level to fetch a light, but after two hours he had still not returned. Eventually the other miner managed to improvise a light. "He went in search of Kellow, and found him lying quite dead and fearfully mutilated on the sollar (landing between ladders) at the 140. In going up the 90 Kellow had to cross a whim shaft over a roadway divided from it by a casing, but it appeared that in endeavouring to find his way in the dark, he went in front of the casing instead of behind it, and so fell down the shaft."

NOTES ON THE NATURAL HISTORY AND GEOLOGY
OF THE POLDICE VALLEY AND ITS SURROUNDINGS

The area is one of great variety, from sheltered valleys to bleak upland moors, from rich farmland to tracts barren for centuries because of toxic minerals, from granite hilltop to marsh, pond, stream and estuary, from dense woodland to thin scrub. For much of the year the Poldice Valley (officially classified as "derelict land") and its southern neighbour, the Consols or Wheal Maid Valley, may at a glance seem like "moon landscape" in contrast with the green island of Goongumpas that divides them, but in fact insects, birds and mammals – particularly rabbits and foxes – are there in profusion, and the plant life is richly varied. Brambles, blackthorn, hawthorn, bracken and gorse flourish, but above all the great swathes of heather (ling and bell heather) are a wonderful sight in late summer – hence my choice of colour for this book's cover. Among the many species of small bird that live and breed in such places are whitethroats, linnets and meadow pipits; ruined engine houses and chimneys make homes for ravens, jackdaws, owls and other birds of prey. Some rare creatures rely on the old mining areas for survival: examples are the greater horse-shoe bat, which spends a third of its life asleep in disused mine workings; and the blue-tailed damselfly, which likes small pools on old mine sites.

Chris Massie has given me the following list of Poldice Valley Flora (just a preliminary one, he says: he hasn't started on the dandelions or grasses yet!). Alder (grey), ash, bay, betony, birdsfoot trefoil, blackthorn, buddleia, Caluna Vulgaris (common heather), campion (white and red), clover (white and red), coltsfoot, cotoneaster (flat and upright types), dogrose, early purple orchid, elm (regenerating naturally at Killicor and Wheal Fortune Farm), Erica Sineria (bell heather), foxglove, greater stitchwort (supposed to be a cure for "the stitch", so a boon for walkers in a hurry), hawthorn, hedera (ivy), hogweed, honeysuckle (several species), hop trefoil, ivy-leaved toadflax, Jacob's-ladder, Japanese knotweed (alas), lousewort, oil seed rape, oxeye daisy, sallow willow, sessile oak, silver birch, silver weed, sorrel, speedwell, stinking iris, sycamore, teasel, three-cornered leek, thrift, valerian, vetch, weald. Bramble, gorse (furze), bracken and other ferns, mosses and lichens could also be added.

Five Cornwall Nature Conservation Sites are within the area covered by the routes in this book: *Restronguet Creek* (saltmarsh and mudflats attracting vast numbers of wading birds, wildfowl and wintering migrant birds) with *Visick's Pool* (reedbed, marsh and wet woodland); the *Lower Carnon River* (fragments of woodland, stretches of gorse and heather, pools supporting dragonflies); *Unity Wood* (ancient oak woodland with rich flora; pond where eleven species of dragonfly have been recorded including three rare or scarce types); *Wheal Busy* (dry heathland plus two pools, again important for dragonflies); and *Wheal Prosper including Tippett's Stamps*, the valley between Chacewater and Twelveheads (mainly dragonflies, too). Two other listed Wildlife Sites are the *Bissoe Valley Nature Reserve* (reclamation of land polluted by arsenic waste, near Point Mills); and *Carn Marth* (pools in old quarries, plus dry heath, grassland and scrub – an important habitat for various mammals, buzzards and kestrels).

* * * *

The creatures and plants that live in the valley have an environment which took millions of years to form. Geological history explains what happened those millions of years ago to cause the development of the tin, copper, wolfram, zinc and other minerals.

In the Devonian era, some 500 million years ago, Cornwall, Devon and Somerset were covered by sea. The sediments deposited on the ocean floor over millions of years were squeezed by pressure of the upper layers to form a slate/shale rock. Cornwall would probably have remained under the sea if a dramatic eruption of the earth's crust had not occurred over a wide area including parts of Brittany. The eruption took place deep below other layers of rock and did not reach the surface like a volcano, but it lifted the slate/shale above sea-level and shattered it, forming great fissures into which fluids and gases from deep in the earth's crust filtered. These cooled and crystallised to form mineral veins, called "lodes" by miners in the South West.

Sometimes the molten lava flowed up into the fissures and formed the whitish rock known locally as "elvan" but which geologists term Quartz Porphyry. The tunnels and bridge abutments at Hale Mills are built of this rock. A great fissure or "dyke" of elvan can be seen on the south side of the southern valley near the old Wheal Virgin engine house. Sometimes because of variations in the mineral content of the lava the fissures were filled with a darker rock technically known as Greenstone but called locally "blue elvan". These fissures vary in size and sometimes individual rock specimens show the effect in miniature whilst other fissures are several yards wide. Archie's Well at Hale Mills (see "Medium Walk B") is quite a stunning example of an open fissure, and there is another nearby at Killicor.

The main body of lava cooled slowly to form the granite for which Cornwall is famous. It exists in Poldice but is still covered by quite a depth of the shale/slate. This, however, is not like the famous Delabole slate which splits so easily and evenly, because at Poldice it has been subjected to great heat and pressure from the granite intrusion. This altered the rock in several ways, examples of which can readily be seen in the waste rock lying around the old mine. The rock was turned plastic by the eruptions and the upthrust caused the shale to become tilted: the horizontal bedding planes were bent, sheared and folded on a massive scale. Such plastic flows can also be seen in small rock samples, and the clifflike sides of the cutting made for the Poldice branch of the Redruth and Chasewater Railway provide a good opportunity to see the effect on a larger scale.

The eruption created spectacular crystal formations which became collectors' items. Scorrier House was reported at one time to possess one of the most extensive collections of minerals in Europe.

All this happened deep underground many millions of years ago. Since then, erosion has removed several thousand metres of shale/slate, so that where once the granite was deep below it is now exposed and forms the high ground of Carn Marth, Carn Brea, Carnmenellis, and, further afield, West Penwith, Bodmin Moor and Dartmoor.

6. A line of granite setts on the Poldice/Portreath Tramway, heading towards Killifreth Mine. The nearest engine houses are Wheal Unity Wood.

7. The Redruth and Chasewater Railway: the bridge under the embankment near Twelveheads
OPPOSITE (Above) 8. The cutting at Hale Mills for the Poldice Branch
       (Below) 9. The "Great Yard", near Carharrack

10. The Hawke's Shaft engine house, Killifreth Mine (Photograph by Chris Massie)

SECTION 4
MAINLY FOR CYCLISTS AND HORSERIDERS

These two routes include some rough and steep sections (particularly number one), and would probably be best suited to those with mountain bikes. They could be linked to form one long ride - or, indeed, one very long walk, but they include a greater proportion on roads than I would normally put into a recommended walk. Many of the points of interest along the way are dealt with in the earlier sections of this book; as for the others, I have space here only to give them brief mention. The directions, too, have to be very concise, and I recommend you to use them in conjunction with the O.S. Pathfinder map (Sheet 1360, Truro). A note about parking is on page 2.

ROUTE ONE :
POLDICE — ST DAY — GWENNAP PIT —
CARN MARTH — LITTLE CARHARRACK — POLDICE

About 5 miles.

The high point, in both senses, of this ride or walk is the splendid view from the top of Carn Marth, but there are many other attractions, such as Gwennap Pit and two good engine houses, both on short diversions from the main route. The first half is almost all uphill and on roads, the second half mostly downhill and on tracks, some of them very rough. There are pubs, shops and toilets at St Day. Fuller details about the area in and around St Day are given under Walk 1; Carn Marth, Pennance Mine, Gwennap Pit and Wheal Grambler/St Aubyn are all featured in A View from Carn Marth, and the last two also in A View from Carn Brea.

1 From Wheal Unity Gate, follow the directions for Walk 2 as far as the T-junction mentioned in point 2, page 28. There turn left, and at the road continue along the track almost opposite, Barracks Lane, into St Day. At the end turn left, then right into Fore Street, past the town clock and the St Day Inn, and down the hill to the Star Inn at Vogue. ("Vogue" comes from a Cornish word meaning furnace or blowing-house, an early form of tin-smelting house.) Just past the pub, fork left on to the minor road to Ninnis and Busveal. A few yards up here on the right is Vogue Shoot or Shute, still much as it was when it supplied water for St Day. (See Paddy Bradley's *A Pictorial History of Redruth & District*, Vol. 2, page 44, for a photograph of the shute in use. "Can you remember," he asks, "the horse drawn water butt that travelled around the district, selling water at 1d a pitcher?") Nearly half a mile beyond that, notice on the left Mynheer Farm, whose name means "long stone"; a plaque fixed to the wall explains why. *(Turn right here for a short diversion to see the fine engine house of Wheal Grambler or St Aubyn United. Return the same way.)* Continue along the road to Busveal, famous as the site of Gwennap Pit, "the Cathedral of Methodism". The Pit is signposted left at the crossroads, but there's another entrance ahead, just past the house on the left. Leaflets and books about the Pit and its links with John Wesley can be obtained at the main entrance or at the house just mentioned.

2 When you are ready to go on, continue up the road in the same direction as before. After about half a mile there is a sharp corner to the right; here

turn left on a minor road. Ignore the first track on the right; go round the left bend, past the circular reservoir, and then up the next track, also on the right. This is stony and quite steep, but don't let that distract you from taking a look at the deep quarry on the left – already being used for storage, and as I write, the subject of a planning application for conversion into an industrial yard. Soon comes the "trig. point" at the top of Carn Marth, one of the best view-points in Cornwall. The ideal time to be here is at dusk on a clear evening, when the lighthouses at St Anthony (near Falmouth) and Trevose (near Padstow) become more obvious than usual, as do the more distant towns such as St Ives and Penzance. Continue beside the flooded quarry; along here, the view to the south and east gets even better. In *A View from Carn Marth* I have quoted the descriptions of this scene written by J.R.Leifchild and George Henwood, both during the 1850s; they make a fascinating comparison with the same panorama today.

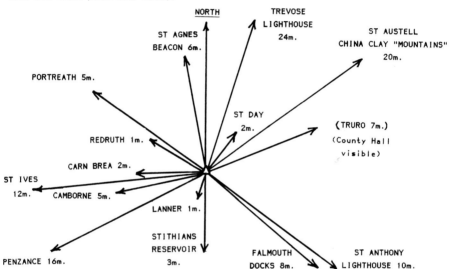

GUIDE TO THE VIEW FROM CARN MARTH
Take your bearings from Carn Brea Castle, due west.

3 *Just beyond the pool, another recommended short diversion: turn right to visit another impressive engine house, that of Pennance Mine. You will also pass another quarry, which has recently been used for theatrical performances by Kneehigh and other groups. Return the same way.* For the main route back to Poldice, turn left instead of right, and keep to this almost straight downhill track for nearly a mile, ignoring side turnings. It's not steep but is very rough in places, with quite big stones, and cyclists in particular need to take special care. You get a fine view over Outer Wood and Carharrack, with Consols and United in the middle distance. At the first road go straight on. At the second, a very narrow one, go left, then first right on another track. Immediately beyond the farmhouse and barn turn right, and at the next road right again. This brings you to a point where several tracks meet on the left. Ignore the one going sharp left, but take the one which passes to the left of the cottages. It curves left; as it starts to bend right towards the Manor House and other houses at Little Carharrack, take the left turning, down to another road via a

small ford with stepping stones. On the ridge ahead is St Day school, and further left at Burnwithian Terrace the former St Day workhouse. Turn right on the road and continue down to the crossroads. Just before that, notice on the left the small old circular building, which in the days before it acquired a corrugated-iron roof was a pound for stray animals.

4 Turn left at the crossroads; please take special care on this busy road. Near the top of the slope, just before you get to the thatched farmhouse (Tresaddern) turn right on the surfaced road signed Wheal Jewell. Soon this becomes a rough track among old mine workings. Bear left, then right along quite a narrow section which widens into a lane at a group of cottages (two of which were called Laurel Cottage and Haldene in 1990). This is Poldice Lane, Crofthandy. At the road, turn left, and soon you reach Crofthandy Methodist Church. Continue along the rough road ahead, Higher Goongumpas Lane, forking left to Crofthandy Gate; the path on the left there brings you back to Wheal Unity Gate.

United Mines District — St. Day in the middle distance.

A 19th-century engraving, reproduced by courtesy of the Royal Institution of Cornwall, showing St Day as seen from a point somewhere near the latter part of Route One. In the centre is the church, probably fairly recently built at the time, to judge by the lack of trees around it. The closest engine house on the right may be on the Wheal Quick section of North Wheal Jewell. Prominent on the left is, presumably, the town's clock tower, but the Consols clock tower does not seem to be shown on the hilltop to the right of the church. Since the artist has added a "romantic" range of mountains – inspired by the china-clay dumps? – perhaps it would be rash to interpret any of the details very literally.

ROUTE TWO: "TAYLOR'S WAY":
POLDICE — WHEAL BUSY — POLDICE — BISSOE —
DEVORAN — POINT AND PENPOL — POLDICE

About 16 miles,
or could be split into several shorter routes.

This is a route covering a huge variety of scenery, much of it very attractive, and crammed with historical interest, following as it does a large part of the course of John Taylor's railway by which the great mines of Chacewater and Gwennap were linked to the nearest south-coast ports. Fuller details about the first part are given under Walk 2, and about the area between Hale Mills and Bissoe under Walk 4; for Devoran, Point, Penpol and other places nearby, see *A View from Carn Marth*. Apart from one optional diversion, the whole route is on roads and bridleways. I must warn horseriders in particular that a short stretch along the very busy A39 is unavoidable unless you omit Devoran, Point and Penpol. The only pub passed is at Devoran, where there are also shops; there is also a shop at Bissoe. With the aid of a map, the long route could easily be divided into various short ones, such as Poldice/Wheal Busy/Poldice, Poldice/Twelveheads or Bissoe or Devoran/Poldice, Bissoe/Devoran/Bissoe, Devoran/Penpol/Devoran.

1 Starting at Wheal Unity Gate, take the tracks across the Poldice Valley to the arsenic works and then go left to leave the valley at Todpool Gate. Turn left on the road through Todpool, and at the crossroads follow the sign ahead to Wheal Bush Farm. Keep to this road now as it climbs past the twin engine houses of Wheal Unity Wood. Later, a short track on the left leads to the restored Old Sump Shaft pumping engine house of Killifreth Mine, and then on the right are the stamps engine house and another chimney of the same mine. At the main Chacewater – Scorrier road, cross with care and continue ahead to visit the arsenic works, engine house and workshops of Great Wheal Busy.

2 From the engine house return to the minor road and go back the way you came for a few yards, but before reaching the arsenic works stack take the track on the right, crossing open heathland. Just after passing a bungalow, go left to the main road, then a few yards left on that, and cross to the track signed Killifreth Engine House. Go along this track to the beautiful Hawke's Shaft pumping engine house (colour photograph 10), then continue along the lane. Soon a gate-cum-stile admits you to Unity Wood, and you have a fairly bumpy ride or walk down through that, among the many old mine shafts. (Don't venture too close to them, or "bumpy" may prove a massive understatement, despite the Clwyd Caps.) Ignore side-paths and tracks to the right; the main track curves left to leave the wood at the valley bottom.

3 *At this point there is a possible diversion, very worthwhile if you are interested in seeing a well-preserved stretch of the Portreath Tramway, the earlier line which competed with Taylor's. This section is not open to horse-riders; cyclists would have to lift their bikes over a gate and then push them for about half a mile. For this route, turn right, so that you have a pool on your left and the wood up on your right. Just before reaching the main St Day – Scorrier road, go sharp left through the narrow opening, manoeuvring your bike as best you can, then walk beside the wall, passing the pond again. This is the tramway route, as the lines of*

granite setts make clear. After about half a mile it brings you to the St Day – Chacewater road. Turn left here, and take the second turning right, signed to Todpool. Pick up the directions at point 4.

Horse-riders, and cyclists wanting the more direct route, turn left, and continue along this track, past a house. At the minor road, turn right, and at the St Day – Chacewater road continue ahead to Todpool.

4 At the left corner in Todpool, turn right through the Todpool Gate at Poldice, then immediately left on the track running down the valley, past Hale Mills to Twelveheads. At the road, continue ahead, and now follow the directions for Walk 4, point 5, page 44. Cross the road and go through the entrance to Cornish Concrete Products. Take the wide track which goes around the edge of the yard, and bear left above the pool and stream. The pool is part of an area now cared for by the Cornwall Trust for Nature Conservation. The tall, tapering stack to the right is a relic of an arsenic works, and the Trust is making valiant attempts to re-vegetate an area whose soil is reputed to have the highest concentration of arsenic anywhere in Europe. The smaller old chimney in the yard of the concrete factory recalls the days when there was a tin streaming and smelting works on this site. Bear left beside the concrete wall, then right. This track, which runs parallel to the old Redruth and Chasewater railway line but west of it, now continues beside the Carnon River all the way down to the A39 near Devoran. It is crossed by three minor roads. At the first one, Bissoe Bridge is a few yards to the right – an attractive old bridge with at least four arches, which can be glimpsed from the track a little further on. This bridge was probably the upper limit of navigation when Bissoe was a port. One patch between here and the next minor road is usually boggy. As you pass under the viaduct carrying the Falmouth branch line, notice the stumps of the original viaduct built for Brunel's Cornwall Railway, which opened in 1863. The line was carried on a wooden superstructure. The GWR took over the Cornwall Railway in 1889 and

Brunel's viaduct over the Carnon Valley, with the Redruth and Chasewater line running beneath it towards Devoran (Reproduced by courtesy of the Royal Institution of Cornwall)

started a programme of replacing Brunel's viaducts with all-stone ones; this one was, I believe, built in the 1920s. The next road you cross was formerly the main Falmouth - Truro turnpike. The old chimney on the left now was once part of a vitriol (sulphuric acid) works, sulphur being a by-product of arsenic refining. This part of the valley has been intensively worked by tin streamers for centuries, and until very recently tin was still being recovered by Carnon Consolidated, owners of Wheal Jane and Mount Wellington. At the date of writing, with tin prices very low, all such work has ceased, and there is talk of developing the area as a golf course and other public amenities. Cross the river by the footbridge, and continue along the gravelled track between fences, which brings you to the A39, Falmouth - Truro road. Cross it with extreme care.

Here you have another choice. If you want to continue to Devoran, Point and Penpol, read on from point 5; for a shorter route, saving about 3 miles, turn right, keeping to the pavement as far as possible, and pick up the directions at point 7.

5 For Devoran, turn left and then first right. Don't turn up Market Street, but continue ahead past the Village Hall and Old Quay House, formerly the Redruth and Chasewater's workshops and offices respectively. At the left corner, go down to the foreshore on the right to see part of the remains of Devoran Quay, which is being restored as a result of local fund-raising, enterprise and effort. Here you will see the eight ruined storage "hutches" used by the mineral railway, and many other relics of Devoran's great days as one of Cornwall's leading ports. More details about all this are in Barry Simpson's book, *Devoran - A Different Cornish Village*, 1990. Return to the road, go round the double bend and continue beside Restronguet Creek along the Old Tram Road, which was the final section of the railway, along which the wagons were drawn by horses even after steam locomotives operated on the rest of the system. The road curves inland a little at Tallack's Creek, on the far side of which it's worth going down the short path on the right to inspect the ruined engine house, dating from about 1824. This is a relic of the Carnon Stream Mine, one of three underwater mines which at different periods worked the alluvial tin on the creek bed. The woods opposite are part of the grounds of Carclew, once the home of the family I have to be careful not to call "the great Lemons" - early mining millionaires. The mansion was burnt down in 1934. About half a mile past the engine house, take the turning on the left - but just before that, notice the well-preserved lime kiln in the small orchard. This is a very good example, and worth a close look. Until very recently the orchard was overgrown and the kiln almost invisible. Continue up to Point village, one of the few in Cornwall with an attractive village green, .complete with old pump. A few years ago it had a shop, too, and long before that a pub, the Bell Inn. Take the next turning right after Point Green, a rough track which was once a ropewalk, as house names confirm. Bear left and at the road turn right down quite a steep hill, past new bungalows, old cottages and a farm to Penpol bridge. This marks the eastern extremity of the route: now the return leg begins.

6 Turn right over a second bridge at the head of Penpol Creek, and continue with the water (or mud) to your left. The first part of Penpol Creek was once a bone-mill pool, and the stepping-stones are on the site of a former tide-mill. On the right after that were lead and tin smelting works, and these marked the terminus of the Redruth and Chasewater Railway. Where

Penpol Creek joins the wider expanse of Restronguet Creek is Point Quay, recently bought, along with the orchard and lime kiln, as a public amenity by Feock Parish Council with the aid of £33,000 raised by the Point Quay Association. Originally Daniell's Quay, it was used during the 19th century for the export of copper ore and the importation of coal and timber for the mines. From here, return to Devoran along the creekside road, as before. At the end of "the Tram", you could go right, up round the hairpin bend to the Old Quay Inn (friendly atmosphere, tasty food) and continue past the attractive houses of St John's Terrace, built in the 1850s mostly for officials of the docks and railway. Turn left down Market Street (formerly Lemon Street), and right at the bottom to return to the A39. There turn left, preferably using the pavement as far as possible.

7 Just past the filling station, cross the road (with great care again) and go along the track or lane which runs beside the Trewedna Stream. On the opposite side is the works known locally as Visick's (pronounced "vie-zix"), but which began in 1858 as the Basset Foundry, doing similar work to its larger neighbour, the Perran Foundry. The remains of a waterwheel dating from 1905 can be seen. Continue past the houses of Tarrandean, bearing right at The Stables. (To the left here is the marshy area known as Mellingey Creek or Visick's Pool.) Eventually you reach the old turnpike road; turn right, then left on the track along which you came earlier. Now it's a matter of retracing your steps (or hoof-marks or wheel-ruts) back to the Poldice Valley; keep right at Hale Mills, but then you could use the track on the left side of the valley, running through the arsenic works at Poldice, and so back to Wheal Unity Gate.

The ruined bob wall, all that remains on surface of the Carnon Stream Mine beside Restronguet Creek. The logs are awaiting use by Ralph Bird, who builds pilot gigs nearby.

FOR THOSE WHO WOULD LIKE TO KNOW MORE

THE STORY OF ENGINES IN POLDICE VALLEY

Before the discovery and harnessing of steam power, the engines at work in Poldice Valley were all driven by water delivered to the valley by leats. Some engines acted as pumps to the mines in the Todpool and Poldice areas and the water discharged down the valley was recycled via a series of waterwheels by entrepreneurial Cornish families: a map in the possession of Lt. Cmdr. Joe Mills of St Day refers among others to "Cap'ns" Phillips, Northey, Tyacks, Francis, Holman and Henry Harris.

The very first considerations given to the introduction of steam power into Poldice Valley were probably in the early 1700s, when two Devonians, Thomas Savery (1650-1715) and Thomas Newcomen (1663-1729) were experimenting with steam power. Newcomen invented the steam-powered "Atmospheric Engine", a machine somewhat more powerful than any produced by Savery, but Newcomen had to build his first engine under the umbrella of Savery's patent and hence approval, which most probably involved some form of royalty payment.

The introduction of steam in Poldice was delayed because of the cost of coal needed to fire the boilers. It was not permitted to sell waste coal, and tax duty on coal was high. When, in 1741, this duty was abolished, Cornwall saw an upsurge in the construction of "Fire Engines", as they were called then. Their introduction at Poldice was almost immediate. Financed by William Lemon, two Newcomen engines were ordered for Poldice Mine, with the aim of using the biggest engine available to pump water from the deep workings to an adit. John Williams was then manager of Poldice and in 1748 he instigated the construction of the Deep Poldice Adit, later called the County or Great Adit: see the note in Walk 4.

By 1777, when four Newcomen engines had been erected at Poldice, new names were becoming important: those of Boulton & Watt, and Joseph Hornblower. Hornblower had been erecting engines in the Midlands for Newcomen before coming to Cornwall and working on his own account. Some details about the three generations of Hornblowers who influenced Cornish engineering history are given in the note on Chacewater (Walk 3).

In 1778 the two Newcomen engines at East Poldice (with cylinders 60" and 66" in diameter) were tested, and their annual coal consumption was estimated as 2,000 tons, a serious drain on adventurers' (shareholders') profits. Boulton & Watt had greatly improve the efficiency of the Atmospheric Engine by introducing a separate condenser, an innovation which Watt patented. So great was the saving in fuel that three 63", 9'-stroke B&W engines were erected at Poldice Mine in 1780, 1782 and 1785. Boulton & Watt astutely contracted to be paid in relation to the savings in fuel costs, and received £2000 per annum for the first three engines. In 1787 a 58" double-acting engine known as Oppy's replaced one of them.

At about this time the adventurers began to realise that the bargain with Boulton & Watt was not as good as first thought, and started to renege on the annual payments. Matters came to a head following what must have been the spectacular destruction of one of the Poldice engines and its house. The *Sherborne Mercury* on the 9th June 1792 reported that apparently two miners smoking pipes in the building had accidentally dropped a spark on a keg of gunpowder, causing this, the first major engine accident to be reported in the press. There was no report from the

Health and Safety! The loss of this engine compounded the already difficult situation: pumping capacity was inadequate and more engines were needed.

At Wheal Unity in December 1793 the erection of a double-cylinder (45" and 53") Hornblower engine was begun. This attracted the attention of Boulton & Watt who made noises about breach of patent but were unwilling to go to court against the well-known Hornblower. In July 1794 the Wheal Unity and Poldice adventurers held a meeting to discuss the erection of a new engine. Boulton & Watt flatly refused to allow the erection of one of their engines while royalties of several thousand pounds were owing to them. With the Hornblowers reluctant to enter into any more contentious situations with Boulton & Watt at this stage, the adventurers turned to Edward ("Ned") Bull, who had been an erector of engines for Boulton & Watt. He had devised an engine with piston set directly over the shaft, thus avoiding the need for the large beam common to all other engines of the day. Messrs J.Williams and J.Martin persuaded Ned to erect the new engine. William Murdock, then the local agent for Boulton & Watt, copied Ned's plans at the Poldice Counthouse and sent them to Watt. The plans were produced in court by Watt in an action for breach of patent, and Ned's engines were found to be a 'manifest piracy'. The court case resulted in the stagnation of engine design and development for years to come and effectively put an end to the great rivalry between Boulton & Watt and Hornblower & Windwood. The latter's engines outstripped B&W's in tests but had not attracted court proceedings from Watt who saw the less well known Bull as an easier target.

1798 saw the erection of a "Rotative Steam Wheel" at Killicor Mine. The curious engine house may well have been built for this engine. The field it stands in is known by locals as Killicor; Wheal Henry was established much later and included Killicor's sett in its workings.

The slump in copper prices early in the 1800s caused a period of inactivity, and many mines were abandoned. But with the revival of prices and the expiry of Boulton & Watt's patent the situation changed dramatically. Improvements in engine design could now be implemented. More efficient engines meant more profits for the mines, which by now were very deep and in constant need of pumping. New engineers began to make their mark; most of the major development from now on was conceived and manufactured in Cornwall, and it is fitting that the machine became known as the "Cornish Beam Engine".

A compound 34" and 60" engine was erected at Wheal Unity in 1816. This was designed by Arthur Woolf (1766-1837), one of a number of brilliant engineers born in Cornwall. Unity was a Williams mine, but Woolf later became Chief Engineer for John Taylor, Williams' great rival, at Consols. John Williams of Scorrier employed William Simms (1762-1834), and Simms and Woolf continued this rivalry in the design and performance of engines. In 1821 Woolf erected 90" engines at Wheal Fortune and Job's Shaft, whilst a Simms 90" was erected at Bissa Pool and two others were erected at Poldice at the restarting of the mine. The *West Briton* of 16th November reported that the pitwork for all three engines had been completed in five months. Simms' Bissa Pool engine outperformed those at Consols in the so-called "Duty" measure. From 1830-50 it was also the hardest worked, doing 12.5 strokes per minute driving the 19" pumps which delivered 887 gallons per minute to the County Adit. In October 1827, however, Woolf's 90" at Wheal Fortune achieved the highest duty of all the engines listed in Lean's *Engine Reporter*.

There must have been a slight downturn in the fortune of mining in the valley in the mid 1830s, as there are reports of James Mitchell of Little Beside auctioning off 60" and 45" engines from Poldice and Wheal Unity, and 1835 saw two other engines sold off.

When Woolf retired in 1833, his able assistants Hocking & Loam took up the practice which he had established, and for a period their claim to be the most eminent engine designers in Cornwall was challenged only by Simms' son, James. During the early 1840s, James Simms was in charge of more engines than anyone else in Cornwall, and topped this creditable position by the invention and later patenting of the Compound Engine.

At this time in Poldice a whim (winding) engine was installed, and in 1844 Pole reported an 80" Bull (inverted) Engine at Creegbrawse Mine, just above Todpool, which was curiously erected "in a House not much larger than itself, the space between the cylinder and walls surrounded in sawdust to preserve the temperature."

Another type of steam engine appeared in the valley after 1856 when Taylor's Redruth and Chasewater Railway converted to steam and two little engines, Miner and Smelter, began work. Soon a third joined them, Spitfire, so called it is said in recognition of the damage to a Mr Tregoning's thatched roof by the sparks from the earlier engines. The company had to rebuild the house with a slate roof as a condition to operating a third engine. The Poldice branch was possibly used only for a short time, because the collapse of the mining industry in Gwennap was not far off.

In 1862 the Todpool shaft engine was sold to Wheal Prudence in Perranporth. In July 1865 work started on Poldice's first Man Engine, at Paynter's shaft, but it was still incomplete when the mine was abandoned in 1867. In 1873 some reworking was attempted. An 85" engine designed by John Hocking was ordered from Perran Foundry at a cost of £2250 complete with boilers. This was the last engine made by the Perran Foundry for the Cornish mines and after only six months was sold when the mine closed yet again. By 1880 all the local mines were closed, apart from West Poldice (formerly Unity Wood) where a 70" engine cast at Harvey's of Hayle in 1860 continued working until 1885, and then again for a short time in 1889.

The valley was now peaceful perhaps for the first time in over 250 years with only the affectionate sounds of the railway engines being heard above Hale Mills. The last train journey to Devoran was made in 1915. Most of the mine engines were bought as scrap by the greatest dealer of the time, J.C.Lanyon & Son. The son Alfred bought all the Poldice engines for £12,000 and those of Clifford Amalgamated for £12,800. The *West Briton* at the time estimated that the latter purchase contained some 100 tons of brass which was fetching 6d (old pennies) a pound. All the scrap was recycled in the usual Cornish manner and made the firm a small fortune.

The waste heaps of Poldice Mine were reworked in a small way, with operations finally closing in 1929; internal combustion rather than steam engines may have been used. Percy Williams of Little Beside is thought to be the last surviving local who worked in the mine.

Nowadays the engine houses at Wheal Unity Wood stand overlooking the western end of Poldice Valley, a reminder of the sights which once must have been. Although engine house remains litter the Poldice and Wheal Unity mines area, those at Killicor or Wheal Henry and Wheal Fortune are the only other substantial surviving examples.

POLDICE VALLEY AND A GREAT MINING BATTLE

No name is more important in the history of Poldice and its mines than Williams. The first members of the family in the valley are said to have been three brothers who came from Wales in the middle of the 17th century. The grandson of one of them, John (I), is one of the most famous of a long line of Williamses who prospered in Cornwall. As manager of the Hearle land in the Manor of St Day, he was well placed to become the most influential mine manager in the area. Successive generations established a dynasty whose supremacy in local mining lasted more than a century. All challenges to it came to nought until the arrival of a young engineer from "up country" in the early 1800s.

John (I)'s grandson, John (II), was appointed manager of Poldice Mine, and his success in the venture of the Deep Poldice (County) Adit and general mine management for the wealthy Mineral Lords in the mid-18th century strengthened the family's already powerful position. The Williamses gave no quarter in the maintenance of that position and in the production of wealth for themselves and their masters. The Deep Adit serves as a good example: virtually overnight it cut off the supplies of surface water that many mills in the valley depended on. Despite the fact that Michael (I) Williams had married Susanna the daughter of Henry Harris of Cusgarne, the Harris mill near Bissa Pool was among those that had to be abandoned.

Michael's son John (III) was, like his father and grandfather, a man of considerable energy and stamina. He bought and enclosed land at Scorrier in 1778, erected Scorrier House and planted the great wood aound it. He was talented and knowledgeable and his reputation was international: Scorrier House was visited by many dignitaries including Louis XVIII and Charles X of France. He appears to have had an insatiable appetite for work, and quite apart from mining interests embracing virtually all of Gwennap and surrounding parishes he still found time to be concerned in the building of the Plymouth breakwater. The 1799 Parliamentary Report on the copper trade noted that he managed no less than 33% of all the mines in Cornwall; some 25 years later many new mines had opened, but 20% of the total was still in the name of Williams. The County Adit was now very extensive, and many mines making payments for adit maintenance recorded payments to "Mr Williams", "John Williams" or simply "Williams". Interests in smelting and shipping were developed as the power base diversified to control whole aspects of mining and metal production. With the Foxes of Falmouth the Williamses constructed and owned the Poldice Tramway (begun in 1809), giving them a virtual monopoly in transport of coal and ore.

No one, it seemed, could challenge this Williams empire, though some tried. Joseph Sowell in 1811 with financial backing from London Gentlemen attempted to re-open United Mines. The response was immediate, and although some 22/64ths of the adventurers supported Sowell the remainder appointed Michael and John Williams as manager and purser following an orchestrated attack on Sowell's ability and integrity. If your face didn't fit you stood little or no chance of making headway: people prospered from business on a grace-and-favour basis, as illustrated by the Williamses' relationship with Collan Harvey of St Day, a brother-in-law of John (III). In partnership with his brother James, Harvey opened a general store in St Day, and the Williamses ordered that all supplies to their mines were to be bought from Harvey's store. Not content with this, Harvey arranged for all miners in Williams mines to be compelled to buy from his store. Miners in Poldice were an unruly lot – for example, they were involved in serious riots in 1787 – and they refused to go to St Day for their purchases when other sources were cheaper. As a result Harvey introduced a "Truck System" whereby miners' pay was reduced if they had not patronised his shop. Local tradition has it that the Harveys dragged a truck around the mines to ensure that they had no excuse for not buying the company's goods. Miners wouldn't "have any truck" either – probably the source of the common expression still in use. *(In fact, of course, the name of the system – common throughout Britain until made illegal by the Truck Acts of 1831 – had nothing to do with trucks, but referred to "trucking" in the sense of bartering.) (B.A.)*

1818 saw a new challenge to the mining supremacy of the Williamses with the arrival of John Taylor at Wheal Fortune, at the east end of the valley.

Taylor was born on 22 August 1779 in Norwich. His mother was related to the powerful Martineau family. He was a devout Unitarian and religion played a prominent part in his life. In 1798 at the age of 19 he was given control by the Martineaus of Wheal Friendship, one of Devon's largest copper mines. He constructed Morwellham Quay and the Tavistock Canal, and by 1808 was controlling nine local mines for the Duke of Bedford. In 1818 he formed a company to re-open the Consolidated Mines in Gwennap, which had already defeated the organisational talents of the Williamses. They had relinquished control through lack of profitability many years before and no doubt viewed this up-country affair with some amusement, expecting it to fail within a few years. The venture was however to become one of the most successful mining operations ever undertaken, producing fabulous wealth and great influence for Taylor. The company was formed from capital of £15,000 together with 100 shares of £650 each subscribed wholly by the London Gentlemen. By mid-1819 the mines had been restored to production and by 1822 their annual output was £80,000-worth of ore, making them the largest producer in Cornwall. By 1837 total production was valued at over £2 million (current value perhaps in the region of £400 million, but such comparisons are hard to calculate), and this success must have galled both the Williamses and the other local adventurers.

To feed the mine with coal and to be able to export the ore without depending totally on the Williams tramway, Taylor obtained an Act of Parliament despite loud objections from the Williamses and built the Redruth & Chasewater Railway. The building of the railway in itself created great local support for the Taylor regime since the Company paid the seemingly generous amount of a shilling for every granite sett delivered, and his Company bought them from all and sundry. Talk of this new face in local mining was, no doubt, plentiful in the gin houses and pubs of the time. The competition between the new line and the Poldice Tramway developed into a rivalry between the Taylor and Williams families which became one of the most titanic power struggles ever seen in the history of mining in Cornwall or elsewhere.

Despite this, Taylor maintained an honest and open approach consistent with his religious convictions. For example, he was not too petty or vindictive to support Williams enterprises when they offered the best product: following early dissatisfaction with the workmanship of Harvey's Hayle Foundry he consistently obtained his engines and other machinery from the Williams foundry at Perranarworthal. Consols and the railway were managed by Taylor on the basis of fair and equal competition, a procedure which antagonised the other mine owners and mineral lords, who were used to being awarded business as a result of their positions of power. Their sense that Taylor posed a threat to their way of business and life was exploited by the Williams family, and the rivalry came to a head in 1836 when Taylor's application for a renewal of his lease of Consols was refused. Taylor subsequently stripped the mine of its available ore, some of which had been stockpiled underground to bolster the Cost Book Company system, the normal way business was operated in those days. It must have galled the onlookers to see such wealth being extracted in the last few years of the lease; and it was perhaps no surprise that the Company's 100 shares were bought by the Williams family for £90,000. They took control in 1840.

From that day, the mine profits gradually fell and production dwindled to a mere quarter of what it had been under Taylor. The rivalry between the families continued, although not with so high a profile as reporters were never allowed to attend the Taylor company meetings, and the attendance of reporters at Williams meetings was strictly manipulated to their own advantage.

Having lost Consols, Taylor was faced with the financial ruin of his railway. The Williamses forced him to reduce drastically the tolls for carrying coal and ore from the Gwennap mines by threatening to use their own tramway or the Hayle Railway, even though the latter's nearest line was still some distance away. Things looked bad for Taylor, and to many it seemed his fate was to be total expulsion from the Cornish mining scene. Unlike Sowell, however, Taylor was a man of considerable means and had influence in high places. He succeeded in acquiring the management of other mines, notably Wheal Buller (between Lanner and Carnkie). Wherever he applied his skills the mines showed profits and despite the cut in tolls on his railway that venture also continued to provide profit for the shareholders. Taylor exercised his influence wherever he could, and new independent managers started to appear for more and more mines at the expense of the Williamses. This subtle change in mine management can be traced back to the middle or late 1830s and was carried out mainly under the protective umbrella of Taylor, who no doubt provided consultancy advice. The Cardozo family were, it seems, also prominent in this attack on the Williams supremacy.

The climax of the power struggle is marked by a number of dramatic events, all concerning the Poldice Valley. During the early 1840s the Williams' control over the running of the County Adit had been partially whittled away as more and more mines, including Creegbrawse, Wheal Busy and some of the North Downs mines, employed their own agents. Responding to this attack, the Williams family diverted all the traffic from United Mines to their own wharf at Devoran, which caused losses in the shipping arm of the Redruth & Chasewater Railway. This was not enough to stem the tide: on 16th July 1853 the family resigned the pursership and management of the Adit after holding them for nearly a century. No accounts exist in records for the Adit below "the separation" (this was the name given to the section from Wheal Andrew to Hale Mills where the first major branch was located). Yet the pursers were responsible not only for the records but also the ordering and purchase of essential material and goods for the upkeep. This included underground clothes, tools and equipment. From 1803 to 1850 this commerce was almost all handled by Collan and James Harvey, although the Foxes of Falmouth also played a part. Interestingly, the Harveys disappear from Adit accounts just prior to the 1853 resignation; whether this resignation was associated with the absence of account records can only be a matter for conjecture. Several associates of the Williams family, notably the Northeys, also suffered a decline in fortunes at about the same time.

Changes were also taking place in the old Taylor regime. John, who by 1850 was 71 years old, passed local control of the railway to his son Richard; but despite the fact that John Taylor & Sons had mining interests worldwide John remained General Manager of the railway: there was no way he was going to relinquish his personal involvement in Cornish affairs.

In the same year as the Williams family resigned their interests in the Adit, the Taylors proposed a new branch line into Poldice, which was later to be extended to Wheal Busy. It was to be driven through the heartland of the Williams mining interests, and the route was to pass very close to the Williams tramway: it seems that the Taylors were intent on absorbing that line to provide a coast-to-coast railway. The branch line had to cross the valley at Hale Mills on a massive embankment with two tunnels, the largest structure on the whole railway. In his work on the railway D.B.Barton states that the elvan used for the tunnel linings was a costly last-minute decision, but this does not seem credible when one considers that the engineers had already driven over 63 miles of tunnel in the mine and excavated a large cutting above Hale Mills Farm years before. They must surely have understood the nature of the shale rock which Barton claims they originally intended to use. Again, the existing structures at Wheal Andrew and above Hale Mills Farm, as well as those on the Tavistock Canal, were constructed in elvan. The Taylors and their engineers knew exactly what they were about when the decision was made to punch the line into Poldice Mine.

The Williams family were not going to take this attack lying down. With their influence in Cornish affairs enhanced by the election of Michael (II) to Parliament in 1853, they arranged for all goods traffic from United and Consols to be shipped down their tramway to Portreath, despite the "altogether wretched" condition of the tramway by that time. Although maps show that Taylor's new steam engines operated as far as Bissa Pool, the branch never proceeded across the valley through Wheal Unity mine, and the secrecy surrounding the matter has shrouded the event in mystery. What is known is that in 1856 the only mine for which the Williamses were now signing was Wheal Unity, directly in the path of the railway.

The struggle between the families ended with the death of John Taylor in 1863 and the sudden demise of the Cornish copper industry at about the same time. The presence of Williams men in mine management increased somewhat in the latter days of Gwennap mining, but their long-standing dominance of mining affairs was never to be recreated.

The Consols clock tower

OTHER BOOKS TO READ

There are, of course, dozens of books about mining and the general history of Cornwall, and a good many of them are mentioned in the preceding pages, but the ones listed below relate particularly closely to Poldice and its immediate neighbourhood.

D.B.BARTON: *The Redruth and Chasewater Railway, 1824-1915* (Bradford Barton, 1960) This 100-page study focuses on "Taylor's Way" but also sets it in a wider context. Everyone "bitten by the bug" of this area will find Barton's book indispensable. Several other books by D.B.Barton are almost equally useful for an in-depth survey, especially *A History of Copper Mining in Cornwall and Devon* and *The Cornish Beam Engine*.

ROGER BURT: *John Taylor, Mining Entrepreneur and Engineer, 1779-1863* (Moorland Publishing, 1977) A brief and readable biography of the man who probably made more impact on this area than any other, and who "had no serious rival" in the mining industry of his time, not only in Cornwall but worldwide.

C.C.JAMES: *A History of the Parish of Gwennap in Cornwall* (no date,but first published in the 1950s) This is a real treasure-store of information, with over 100 pages on geology and mines. It is out of print, but copies are readily available in local libraries.

A.K.H.JENKIN: *Mines and Miners of Cornwall*, Part VI: Around Gwennap (1963; reprinted 1981) The classic brief study of this mining area, including some interesting old drawings, photographs and maps.

DAVID WISEMAN: *The Fate of Jeremy Visick* (1981; Puffin Books 1984) The central characters of this story are two 12-year-old boys, and it is aimed at readers of about that age, but can equally be enjoyed by adults. The main settings are Gwennap village and Wheal Maid, and the author vividly conjures up Consols, United and Poldice as they were in the 1850s and as they are now. He portrays well the daily lives of Cornish miners and the dangers they faced.

DAVID WISEMAN: *Jumping Jack* (1988; Yearling Books, paperback, 1989) This story for younger children is less specific in its setting, but when we read that one of the characters fell down a mine shaft near "the old clock tower" we naturally think of Consols again. Young readers of this one will be unlikely to stray from the paths!

The *Mineral Tramways Project* report published by the Cornwall Archaeological Unit in 1990 is a fascinating and attractively-presented document, packed with useful information and imaginative proposals for the preservation and benign exploitation of Cornwall's central mining region. Finally, I won't allow modesty to forbid mention of three earlier books of my own (numbers 1, 2 and 6 in the Landfall Walks Books series listed opposite), which suggest a total of 28 walks within a radius of about ten miles of Poldice: a practical, enjoyable (and even healthy!) way of setting the topic of this book within a wider historical context.